371.
826
60971
SHO

Making the case
2SLGBTQ+ rights and
religion in schools

MAKING THE CASE

MAKING THE CASE

2SLGBTQ+
Rights and Religion in Schools

DONN SHORT

BRUCE MacDOUGALL

PAUL T. CLARKE

Copyright © 20.. n imprint of UBC Press

All rights reserved. No p... tion may be reproduced, stored in a retrieval system, or t... form or by any means, without prior written permission of the publisher, or, in Canada, in the case of photocopying or other reprographic copying, a licence from Access Copyright, www.accesscopyright.ca.

371.826 60971 SHO

Purich Books, an imprint of UBC Press
2029 West Mall
Vancouver, BC, V6T 1Z2
www.purichbooks.ca

30 29 28 27 26 25 24 23 21   5 4 3 2 1

Printed in Canada on FSC-certified ancient-forest-free paper (100% post-consumer recycled) that is processed chlorine- and acid-free.

Library and Archives Canada Cataloguing in Publication

Title: Making the case : 2SLGBTQ+ rights and religion in schools / Donn Short, Bruce MacDougall, and Paul T. Clarke.

Names: Short, Donn, author. | MacDougall, Bruce, 1960- author. | Clarke, Paul Terence, 1960- author.

Description: Includes bibliographical references and index.

Identifiers:
Canadiana (print) 2021030054X | Canadiana (ebook) 20210300574 | ISBN 9780774880701 (hardcover) | ISBN 9780774880718 (softcover) | ISBN 9780774880725 (PDF) | ISBN 9780774880732 (EPUB)

Subjects: LCSH: Sexual minority students—Civil rights—Canada. | LCSH: Sexual minority students—Legal status, laws, etc.—Canada. | LCSH: Educational law and legislation—Canada. | LCSH: Religion in the public schools—Canada. | LCSH: School environment—Social aspects—Canada.

Classification: LCC LC2576.C3 S56 2021 | DDC 371.826/60971—dc23

UBC Press gratefully acknowledges the financial support for our publishing program of the Government of Canada (through the Canada Book Fund), the Canada Council for the Arts, and the British Columbia Arts Council.

Printed and bound in Canada
Set in Akzidenz-Grotesk and Devanagari by Artegraphica Design Co.
Copy editor: Andrew Wilmot
Proofreader: Helen Godolphin
Indexer: Emily LeGrand
Cover designer: Jess Koroscil

FOR CHLOE

Contents

Acknowledgments / viii

Introduction: Journeys / 3
Donn Short

1 Legal Possibilities / 20

2 The Safe and Welcoming School / 45

3 Voices That Matter / 62

4 "What's New?" / 84

5 Making Spaces, Making Community / 102

Conclusion: Getting There / 126

Notes / 135

Bibliography / 147

Index / 153

Acknowledgments

The authors would like to thank Adam Gingera, Steve Falkingham, Jonathan Andrews, Reid Buchanan, Jack Powles, and David Barbour for providing research assistance. Many thanks to Matthew Renaud in the Robson Hall E.K. Williams Law Library. The staff of the Law Library at the University of British Columbia were, as always, unfailingly helpful. The authors also gratefully acknowledge the support of the Legal Research Institute of the University of Manitoba and the Manitoba Law Foundation.

MAKING THE CASE

INTRODUCTION

Journeys

••• DONN SHORT •••

A SINGLE STEP

It is said that every journey begins with a single step. Isabella Burgos was about to take a giant leap.

Isabella Burgos, or "Bella," knew exactly who she was. She had spent the summer of 2014 defining – for herself and her family – her sense of self, her identity as an eight-year-old transgender girl. When school began again in September, Bella planned to take another giant leap and affirm her identity publicly and very bravely.

For 2SLGBTQ+ students, the first step is self-awareness – acknowledging to themselves who they truly are. That process can be difficult enough. Acknowledging who they are to others – particularly friends at school, classmates who may prove less than friendly, and teachers – is fraught with challenges and, sometimes, danger as their identities may not fit within traditional social norms and expectations.

Even within their own families, 2SLGBTQ+ students often are at risk. Ideally, for most children and youth, their parents, grandparents, brothers, and sisters can be a source of support during adolescence; however, for many 2SLGBTQ+ students, their identities may, in fact, be a source of stress or conflict within the family.[1]

The term "coming out" refers to a lifelong process of the personal and public development of a positive gay, lesbian, bisexual, or transgender identity. For many 2SLGBTQ+ individuals, the first public step in declaring who they are begins at school. And increasingly, students are coming out earlier and in greater numbers than ever before;[2]

however, many struggle first with their own negative self-perceptions, stereotypes, and feelings of homophobia and/or transphobia learned and internalized while growing up.

Coming out, acknowledging one's identity, can be a very freeing and empowering experience for 2SLGBTQ+ students. Doing so allows them to live more honest lives and develop genuine trust and relationships with others. That said, the process is often one of both risks and rewards as acknowledging one's true self can be and sometimes is perceived as a threat to others and to one's community.[3] While the rewards include building self-esteem and confidence and connecting with other 2SLGBTQ+ individuals, the risks – permanently changed relationships and potentially opening oneself up to rejection, discrimination, harassment, and/or physical abuse – are equally great.

Initially, Bella's experience at her school was positive. Adults changed that.

On the first day of school in 2014, and for a few days afterwards, Isabella used the girls' washroom at her elementary school in River East Transcona School Division (RETSD) in Manitoba without incident. In fact, Isabella told her parents that her friends and classmates had been supportive of this. Isabella felt safe.

Unfortunately, during the second week of September, the school's principal saw Isabella leaving the girls' washroom and told her she was not allowed to use it again. A few days later, a classmate's mother, who happened to be nearby, observed Isabella coming out of the girls' washroom and confronted her, telling Isabella that she could not use that washroom. This parent conveyed these same sentiments to Elizabeth Burgos, Isabella's mother, referring to Bella with male pronouns in the process.

Elizabeth Burgos and her husband Dale had conversations about this with the school, but the principal steadfastly refused to let Bella use the girls' washroom, insisting that she instead use the individual washrooms located throughout the school. However, it was never the expectation of Bella's parents that Bella would use only the individual washrooms, but that they would be available to her whenever she felt unsafe or needed to use them.

For Isabella and her parents, this single option was not good enough. Not only did it segregate Bella from her classmates, it also relayed to others an unacceptable, harmful, and discriminatory message. Bella wanted the option to use the individual washroom, but she also sought the option to use the same washroom as any other girl in her school.

By the third week of September, Isabella's parents had decided to keep her home from school. They did not want her to experience segregation by being refused the right to continue to use the girls' washroom. Several days later, however, Bella returned to school because she wanted to be with her friends. The school continued to permit her to use only the individual washrooms and not the girls' washrooms. The negative impact on Isabella's well-being was noticeable and deeply felt.

Unable to shift the principal's position and concerned for her daughter's safety, largely due to the bullying by another student's mother, Elizabeth Burgos filed a human rights complaint against RETSD.

The complaint alleged, among other things, that RETSD, contrary to section 13 of the *Human Rights Code*, had discriminated against Bella in the provision of a service on the basis of her gender identity (transgender female) and/or failed to reasonably accommodate her special needs based upon her gender identity (transgender female) without bona fide and reasonable cause.

In essence, Bella was being denied the right to be who she was.

And so began Bella's very public journey. Her quest to full selfhood and citizenship received national attention and lasted almost two years. Like all journeys, there would be a cost to it, but also, in time, an end and – as is happening more and more frequently for 2SLGBTQ+ students like Bella – victory.

ASKING DIRECTIONS

"How do we get there?" I asked the student at the front door of the school.

A simple question but also a metaphor for what followed. I was in Toronto attending a student-run conference with a colleague. The conference was addressing the issue of sexual orientation and bullying. I was trying to find the auditorium where presentations were being given.

These were my first steps into work that would provide the basis for my career, and that would eventually give rise to my initiating this book. In retrospect, that simple request for directions strikes me now as indicative of the larger question animating both my work and that of the authors of this book:

How do we create safe and inclusive schools for 2SLGBTQ+ youth? What's stopping us?

When it comes to the safety of 2SLGBTQ+ youth, students and teachers favour a broad definition of the term: safety must mean the inclusion and celebration of all students, regardless of identity. Often this is in conflict with the larger school culture, which frequently shows itself to be uncaring and/or hostile toward 2SLGBTQ+ students.

This is not likely to change when policies that exist to deal with bullying are conceptualized as "incident-bound" and "responsive" to isolated incidents. No matter how immediately or effectively punitive measures may be brought to bear on bullies, said punishments do nothing to change the current climate of a school system that gave rise to such harassment, marginalization, and bullying in the first place.

Eradicating bullying on its own is not enough. It is an effective starting point, but it is not where we want to end up. Schools must recognize, support, and celebrate its 2SLGBTQ+ students. Transforming the very culture of our schools is the only way to achieve "safe schools" for all 2SLGBTQ+ youth.

That is where we want to "get to."

And the journey to that point contains two key elements: policies and education.

ROAD BLOCKS

So, what *is* stopping us?

Much of the resistance to creating safe and inclusive schools comes from the perceived impossibility of the task at hand. In particular, there is the perception that making schools safe for 2SLGBTQ+ students conflicts with the religious rights of others.

Other students, teachers, parents all have rights, too, don't they? Yes, they do. Those rights, particularly freedom of religion, have been recognized for decades, if not hundreds of years. But 2SLGBTQ+ students have rights, too, and those rights have been of concern for a much shorter period of time.

Students who are 2SLGBTQ+ have the right to go to school free from discrimination; they have the right to full citizenship in the schools they attend. So perhaps it was inevitable that there would be clashes between these two sides. And it is predictable that conflicts between 2SLGBTQ+ youth and their allies on the one hand, with so much more work to do, and those claiming religion-based rights on the other, who often – but not always – view that work as an infringement on their own rights, are going to continue.

The simple truth is, creating safe, inclusive schools is possible. Some schools are there already. For others, it will be a journey. But the results of legal challenges based on religious rights claims have increasingly resulted in wins for 2SLGBTQ+ rights.

Over the past twenty-five years, both lawmakers and the courts have sided with the desire to create safe and inclusive spaces for 2SLGBTQ+ students. The preconception that changing the culture of schools is impossible is just that – a preconception. It is possible, it has already been happening, and it will continue. The question for our times is: what role does each of us have in furthering that change?

Our goal with this book is to demonstrate this new truth, this new reality for 2SLGBTQ+ kids in school.

The law is on their side.

The law is on the side of those who support them.

So how do we get there with school culture itself? The first step is to recognize that laws aimed at responding to specific incidents of violence against 2SLGBTQ+ youth are insufficient. No matter how vigorously disciplinary measures are enforced, they are consistently shown to be ineffectual at preventing discrimination and violence aimed at 2SLGBTQ+ youth.[4] What is needed are policies and educative initiatives that seek to transform the larger hostile culture of schools.

Secondly, it must be noted that some 2SLGBTQ+ individuals experience multiple forms of oppression. This is true, for example, of 2SLGBTQ+ students who are also Indigenous. Making safe and inclusive schools means also acknowledging and responding to the ways in which schools have failed these students, in particular with respect to their multiple identities.

Intersectionality is a framework for understanding how an individual's multiple social positions (e.g., sexuality, gender, sex, disability,

● ● ● ● ● ● ● ● ● ●
HOMOPHOBIA

Once used to refer to a culturally produced fear of homosexuality. More often used in a modern sense to indicate an intense dislike, distaste, or hatred of homosexuality and persons who are 2SLGBTQ+ or perceived to be. This dislike or hatred also includes biphobia, transphobia, acephobia, and just general queerphobia.
● ●

race, class) combine to create several modes of discrimination and privilege.⁵ Only by understanding the interconnected nature of, for instance, race, class, and gender (e.g., an Indigenous woman living in poverty) as they apply to an individual or group can we begin to comprehend the day-to-day experiences of an individual who intersects with more than one of these categories. In addition to Indigenous students, a 2SLGBTQ+ student with disabilities will experience school differently than a 2SLGBTQ+ student without disabilities.

Intersectionality requires that we identify and respond to the multiple forms of message giving and receiving that happens in schools intersecting with these individuals, to heed the possibility that some may experience disadvantage and inequality in more than one way.

● ● ● ● ● ● ● ● ● ● ● ● ●
INTERSECTIONALITY

Intersectionality is a framework for understanding the ways in which multiple forms of inequality or disadvantage converge in an individual's lived experiences. For example, a 2SLGBTQ+ student with disabilities experiences school differently than a 2SLGBTQ+ student without disabilities. This is true also of students who are Indigenous or assigned female at birth. An awareness of the intersection of these different modes of discrimination and privilege helps us to address the multiple failures in law and other social justice movements in achieving full social justice.
● ●

A long history of targeting Indigenous communities has contributed to how Indigenous youth experience discrimination and harassment at school from both students and staff. To that end, empirical evidence exists illustrating that approximately 65 percent of Indigenous 2SLGBTQ+ students feel unsafe at school because of their sexual orientation, 51 percent because of their gender expression, and 19.7 percent because of their race or ethnicity.[6] Furthermore, Indigenous 2SLGBTQ+ students have reported harassment or assault at school based on their sexual orientation (78.4 percent), gender expression (70.4 percent), and/or race/ethnicity (46.1 percent).[7]

These results confirm that Indigenous 2SLGBTQ+ students experience school at the intersection of their racial identity, gender, and sexual orientation. It is therefore clear that in order to address the needs of Indigenous 2SLGBTQ+ students, schools must adopt an intersectional approach that challenges homophobia, transphobia, and racism.[8]

The same study confirmed the positive impact on the day-to-day experiences of Indigenous 2SLGBTQ+ students when schools have in place supportive resources, such as gay-straight alliances, sometimes called gender-sexuality alliances or GSAs, ethnic/cultural clubs, and specially trained teachers and staff.[9]

It makes sense then to champion laws and policies that give greater visibility to, and acceptance and celebration of, all 2SLGTBTQ+ students in their various identities. In short, these students deserve to have full citizenship in the schools they attend – just like everybody else.

Let's rethink the preconceptions that defeat us before we even begin.

BIG IDEAS, BIG CHANGE ... BIG CONFLICT?

Is conflict inevitable when students need or want to be who they are? If legislation and policies are reconceptualized to transform school culture, to embrace and celebrate all students regardless of identity, their effectiveness will be greater. Students and teachers alike want to believe in the possibility that the larger school culture can change, and as more and more changes occur, this possibility will eventually become reality.

But there will be resistance at each step along the way. Often it will be expressed via religious concerns or similar language; however, opposition to change will not always be grounded in religious objection, and religion-based objections do not exist within a vacuum. Rather, they exist as a powerful, defiant front resulting from larger cultural change. Some people, like the mother at Bella Burgos's school, are afraid of the larger cultural change they see happening all around them. The faces on TV are not the same as they used to be. Marriage does not look like it once did.

As society moves forward and culture changes with it, power shifts into different hands. The influence of religion-based rights, for example, which previously seemed unlimited in scope, has been revealed to be far more limited than many would have thought, with historically unchallenged cultural spaces being more frequently disputed.

And so, at this juncture, most of the resistance to cultural change, in and out of schools, will be grounded in religious objection. Therefore, competing rights scenarios will arise with greater frequency.

It is fair at this point to ask what a competing rights scenario looks like. How will we know when different sets of rights compete with each other? And how will that competition be resolved?

A competing rights claim occurs when legally protected rights are present in claims made by two individuals or groups; however, a competing rights claim does not necessarily create a conflict with the *Charter*[10] or result in unconstitutionality.

COMPETING RIGHTS

Sometimes a rights claim made by one person will conflict, or appear to conflict, with a rights claim made by someone else. This can happen when a 2SLGBTQ+ student asserts their right to exist free from discrimination inflicted by a teacher or another student, who in turn complains that the 2SLGBTQ+ student's identity violates their legally protected religious freedoms. If possible, the courts will try to accommodate both rights claims. Sometimes, however, that is not possible. In such cases, the courts will then ask if the 2SLGBTQ+ rights claim infringes on the religion-based right in a significant way. If the answer is no, the religion-based claim will give way to the rights claim.

The Supreme Court of Canada has developed a framework for dealing with competing rights.[11] The court has said that rights claims should first be reconciled, if possible, through accommodation, but if competition is inevitable, claims must then be reconciled through balancing those rights currently in competition.[12]

The impact on both rights must be discerned, and balancing competing rights claims must be approached on a case-by-case basis. The analysis is deeply contextual, looking at the facts of actual conflicts and the *Charter* and constitutional values at stake. There is no one-size-fits-all solution to responding to conflicting rights claims.

Overall, the courts will endeavour to respect both sets of rights. If, however, there is no way to accommodate both rights, then and only then can rights be held to be in collision.

SEX AND RELIGION MERGE

Two parts of society that have become more complex in recent years – in terms of increasing recognition and influence – are sexuality[13] and religion.[14] However, through the power and influence of the media (including social media), television, movies, and music, traditional presumptions of heteronormativity (that heterosexuality is the default for most people) and assumptions about the primacy of Christianity have given way to a more nuanced understanding of religious and sexual diversity in Canada. This change has also been reflected in the law – courts have shown a willingness to rethink conventional perspectives that have, up to now, defined the structure and content of what is taught in schools. Further, lawmakers and the courts, in rethinking these perspectives, have exhibited a willingness to target the culture of schools. In short, those of us who undertake this change are not alone – the law supports us.

More recently, legal challenges have expanded to include sexualities and identities, on the one hand, and religion-based claims on the other. This book, therefore, considers how identities, sexualities and religion are increasingly coming into overt competition with one another. While most legal disputes so far have involved sexuality claims, we look at how legal claims related to identities and sexualities, newly or recently recognized in law, have succeeded in finding a foothold and increasing success in an education system in transition.

These issues are examined through both legal and educational lenses. Law and education are both normative enterprises that help to shape and mould human conduct. They do this by conveying certain accepted values and norms. It is not possible to separate one from the other.

Educational systems – both public and denominational – operate within a legal system that requires certain standards be met. In addition, the law requires that schools recognize various rights. The law supports 2SLGBTQ+ students on the basis that they are entitled to equality, and to attend school free from discrimination.

This protection comes from different legal sources. The constitutional basis for the guarantee of equality comes from the *Canadian Charter of Rights and Freedoms*. The *Charter*, finalized in 1981, enacted in 1982 – although the section 15 equality provisions did not come into effect until 1985 – is now part of the *Constitution Act* that created Canada in 1867. The *Charter* restricts government action and the actions of those to whom government delegates its authority – such as schools.

Section 15 guarantees equality before and under the law and equal protection and benefit of the law regardless of one's race, national or ethnic origin, colour, religion, sex, age or mental or physical disability. These are known as the "enumerated grounds."

2SLGBTQ+ persons are not specifically mentioned in section 15. However, the Supreme Court of Canada has held that section 15

●●●●●●●●●●●●●●●

HETERONORMATIVITY

Heteronormativity is a system of attitudes based on cisgender expectations promoting heterosexuality as the normal and expected sexual orientation for both men and women. When the math teacher gives her students an algebra problem involving husband, Abhi, and wife, Isha, she may be racially sensitive, but her example is heteronormative.

Heteronormativity refers to the privileging of heterosexuality and the marginalizing of 2SLGBTQ+ people in the institutions of the family, health care, schools, marriage, media, and the workplace.

●●●●●●●●●●●●●●●●●●●●●●●●●●●●●●●●●●●●●

protection includes certain "analogous grounds," including sexual orientation.

2SLGBTQ+ students derive protection from human rights legislation that exists in each province and territory in Canada. For example, in Ontario, the *Human Rights Code* recognizes and protects students (or anyone) from discrimination based on their sexual orientation and gender identity and gender expression. The legislation differs somewhat between the individual provinces and territories (some statutes expressly protect gender identity and gender expression), but human rights statutes are considered quasi-constitutional, meaning they take priority over any other provincial laws.

Protection is given also to religion-based rights claims. These rights also find their basis in both constitutional and human rights-based protections (see Chapter 2). Certain claims to religious education, such as the separate status of Roman Catholic schools in Ontario, are also subject to constitutional protection under the *Constitution Act, 1867*.

GAY-STRAIGHT ALLIANCES

Decisions by school authorities in support of 2SLGBTQ+ students inevitably upset certain religious groups and persons. This is especially true in recent debates regarding the mandating of gay-straight alliances or gender-sexuality alliances (GSAs) in Canadian schools.

Strong reactions have resulted from the debates around GSAs as it is often argued that sexual orientation rights conflict with the freedom of religion of others. This is almost always the argument asserted by someone objecting to the establishment of a GSA in a particular school.

However, human rights tribunals and Canadian courts have continually held that protecting freedom of religion should not be grounded in the exclusion of 2SLGBTQ+ students or the denial of the rights of 2SLGBTQ+ students to be safe and free from discrimination in schools.

This has been the law's journey.

In recent years, Ontario, Manitoba, and Alberta introduced legislation permitting GSAs. These provinces compelled schools to establish GSAs when requested by students, and gave students the right to use the word "gay" in the name of the group.

There was both support and, predictably, objections.

Those objections remind us that defending the human rights of 2SLGBTQ+ students will inevitably occur alongside assertions that sexual orientation rights are in conflict with religion-based claims and religious exceptionalism. These objections can be counted on when crafting legal responses to homophobic and transphobic bullying in schools.

Certainly, religion-based resistance will be mounted in opposition to the transformative goals of these positive and inclusive approaches. These sorts of objections will continue until the day comes when 2SLGBTQ+ acceptance is the norm.

That day will come.

OTHER QUESTIONS

The debates surrounding GSAs have proven to be foundational to other disputes and have given rise to other questions. For example, can a religion-based school exclude 2SLGBTQ+ students?

This very question created a national furor when Trinity Western University in British Columbia (TWU)[15] announced its intention to create a new law school. Trinity Western University proposed that its students be required to sign a controversial community agreement, or covenant, that included abstinence from sex outside of heterosexual marriage.

Eventually, the Supreme Court of Canada said no.

HETEROSEXISM

Heterosexism is the assumption that everybody is heterosexual. It is an example of prejudice, stereotyping, or discrimination against 2SLGBTQ+ persons, and is grounded in the belief that heterosexuality is "normal," and that same-sex relationships and same-sex sexual activity and desire are outside the norm.

Heterosexism then is a bias, prejudice, or viewpoint that favours heterosexuals.

The court was confronted with two competing rights claims. The rights of 2SLGBTQ+ students were pitted against TWU's claim to operate within its religious mandate.

Trinity Western University's self-stated mission was "to develop godly Christian leaders: positive, goal-oriented university graduates with thoroughly Christian minds; growing disciples of Jesus Christ who glorify God through fulfilling the Great Commission, serving God and people in the various marketplaces of life." In weighing the two claims, the court decided that it was "proportionate and reasonable" to limit religious rights as stated in the school's mission statement in order to ensure open access for 2SLGBTQ+ students.

These debates should not lead anyone to conclude that 2SLGBTQ+ students do not have allies among the religious in public schools or even in denominational schools. When debates in Ontario were raging about the proposed GSA legislation, OECTA (the Ontario English Catholic Teachers' Association) voiced unwavering support for the new law. The trustees of denominational schools and bishops strongly objected.

Many of their objections were grounded in mistaken beliefs as to what the law says regarding the scope of religion-based rights claims. There has been, for too long, particularly in public discourse and among religionists, a mistaken belief in the sacrosanct or exclusive management rights of Roman Catholic school boards to "run their own show." This attitude has led to the mistaken view that strength of religious conviction in some way justifies ignoring (or indeed permitting) the harassment of 2SLGBTQ+ students within the Roman Catholic school system. That view is not supported in law.

Do the equality rights claims of 2SLGBTQ+ students diminish, to any extent, the right to freedom of religion of others? Or the rights of religions as a whole? Can a religion-based school limit 2SLGBTQ+ presence within its culture and extracurricular activities?

If there is concern that religious expression must be protected, what constitutes that religious expression? Does its protection require the elimination or suppression of other voices? To what extent can religious beliefs be brought into secular-based schools by trustees, principals, and teachers?

To answer these questions, and the question of whether or not religion-based rights claims have been given singular treatment in law when compared with the rights of other protected groups, various claims must be looked at.

That question challenges preconceptions. Contesting well-established beliefs prompts additional inquiry: What role do preconceptions serve? Why the recourse to preconceptions?

On a broad level, it might be argued that such fixed conceptions are necessary in order to have a uniform approach to rights. But in what ways are fixed conceptions a disservice to 2SLGBTQ+ students? Are fixed conceptions not also harmful to new religions?

These are the inquiries to be made in the face of schools being transformed by "the new" – by 2SLGBTQ+ students who are out and demanding to be included, and who have the law on their side. The question might be asked, "What is new?" Legal recognition usually lags behind cultural recognition – which itself is often behind, both in terms of recognizing and valuing and embracing, that which actually has been present all along.

Accommodation of rights has largely been the answer in the conflict between sexual orientation claims and religion-based claims – that things are fine the way they are, and that there are only a few, rare "problems" or "issues" that accommodation finds difficult to resolve.

But there can be a different approach.

The best way to confront and accept the inevitable truth – that schools must be transformed – lies in the empowerment that comes from the fact that religion-based rights claims, which traditionally have been given almost unfettered primacy, are now compelled to make space for the sexual orientation claims of 2SLGBTQ+ students.

This view is not radical or even new.

The requirement for freedom of religion to give way to the protection and rights of others has always been a part of freedom of religion as defined by the Supreme Court of Canada. With this knowledge in hand, initiatives to transform schools by targeting bullying, marginalization, and heteronormativity can be discovered.

WHAT'S INSIDE?

At all stages, the importance of inclusionary and empowering strategies over attitudes of exceptionalism and privilege is key. That is the argument you will find in this book.

Chapter 1, "Legal Possibilities," assesses how contention has risen in the context of education, and what legal factors are appropriate in reaching a resolution.

Chapter 2, "The Safe and Welcoming School," focuses on how initiatives in one particular area – bullying – were challenged, ultimately succeeding in the implementation of 2SLGBTQ+-supportive policies.

Chapter 3, "Voices That Matter" identifies what voices need to be heard in discussions, debates, and litigation surrounding education issues, especially the voices of children, who have often been silenced or subsumed by the voices of others.

Chapter 4, "'What's New'?" underscores the need to recognize that the face of Canada is changing or being seen for what it truly is for the first time. This change is unsettling for the status quo in schools and other aspects of Canadian society.

Chapter 5, "Making Spaces, Making Community," and the Conclusion, "Getting There," deal with more specific ways to ensure that all relevant voices in this contentious matter are heard. They address factors to consider when developing both a school and a curriculum inclusive of those people and voices.

This is the challenge of finding spaces for – what is for the law – "new" voices and people. Point of fact, these individuals and identities have actually been present all along. What is "new" is that the law and schools are only now recognizing and respecting them.

This journey is intended to be of use in formulating approaches to help resolve these issues. Taking the trip requires one to question their assumptions about how schools work and whose voices matter. How these questions get resolved may vary from school to school, but the considerations giving rise to change remain factors that all schools have in common.

BELLA ECSTATIC

The Burgos family had hoped to reach an agreement with the School Division instead of going to a hearing.[16] In 2016, after eighteen months,

RETSD agreed to a settlement. As part of the agreement, the School Division made revisions to its guidelines to provide greater clarity and to add emphasis for the rights of transgender students and staff. They also agreed to provide training to teachers and staff. Employing a rights-based approach to gender inclusion, the guidelines acknowledged that transgender students were entitled to equal rights.

Elizabeth Burgos was aware that the entire country was following her family's journey to equality: "This complaint has been followed closely by many across the country who were anxious to learn how the Division would respond to this issue. Our goal was to ensure that there was better education around the rights of transgender individuals. We are very pleased that our ongoing discussions ... have resulted in a tool that others can adopt so transgender students and staff feel protected and welcomed in their communities."[17]

It is interesting to remember that the so-called threat to the school in this case was perceived by a parent, and that the human rights complaint was made following an instance of bullying by the mother of another student. Bella's friends and classmates had, in fact, accepted her.

Elizabeth Burgos summed up the case this way, "We had three goals going in – that was education, training and trans rights guidelines. We got all three. For us, it's a win."[18]

Bella's journey lasted almost two years. At its conclusion, her mother confirmed that "Bella is doing great. She is ecstatic. We're celebrating just having that connection and moving forward, just knowing such goodness came out of a long year and a half."[19]

DISCOVERING YOURSELF

You will recognize yourself or your school in this book.

It is a truism that schools matter. What happens in school, when it happens, and who decides what happens are perpetual subjects of discussion and contention.

While these issues have been the subject of debate in the community – and still are – they have been also the subject of legal disputes. In most of the related high-profile legal cases, there has been an opposition of claims based on minority sexuality and claims based on religion.

For years, many 2SLGBTQ+ people have lived with limitations imposed on their day-to-day lives by the constraints of law. Children and youth, in particular, have appeared in law as legal objects rather than legal subjects – property rather than persons. They have been acted upon rather than being treated as actors themselves.

Presented here are the new kids in school. Their new legal identities offer transformative possibilities toward the creation of safer, more inclusive, more welcoming schools and new ways of conceptualizing sexuality, gender and religion.

This book is for them and the people who support them.

This book is for you.

1
Legal Possibilities

NEW FACES

Grade 11 student Evan Wiens was the only openly gay student at Steinbach Regional Secondary School in Manitoba. He was a frequent victim of bullying in his school and was not being supported by school administration.

But Evan was more than a victim. He was also a son, a friend, and a student, and in 2013, part of a rising group of student-led activism that can now be found in many schools – even in some surprising places. Like Steinbach, for example, a city of strong Mennonite influence located an hour's drive southeast of Winnipeg, home to fewer than fifteen thousand people.

In 2013, the NDP provincial government introduced *Bill 18*[1] – an anti-bullying bill with particular concern for 2SLGBTQ+ students. The proposed legislation dealt with bullying on school property, including bullying that took place after school hours and cyberbullying. In particular, *Bill 18* underscored the school's responsibility to deal with bullying and to create a discrimination-free environment for 2SLGBTQ+ students.

The proposed legislation required accommodation of students who wished to promote awareness of various sexual orientations and gender identities. In particular, the bill mandated that schools permit student groups to use the name "gay-straight alliance" or "gender-sexuality alliance," or "GSA" or an equivalent, to promote a positive and inclusive environment.

Clubs occupy influential positions in schools. And names matter – the Chess Club, the Math Club, and the Drama Club take pride in both their activities and their names; however, when it comes to a GSA, some schools are more comfortable, and agreeable, to the creation of a GSA in the first place providing the name of the club is vague.

Even the Diversity Club downplays and, in fact, renders invisible the 2SLGBTQ+ students in the group.

Studies have shown that "generic" approaches to inclusion do not work.[2] Unless 2SLGBTQ+ students are specifically identified in school proposals designed to champion their identities and help end their marginalization and harassment, then their specific needs are missed, forgotten, or avoided, their status as "other" remaining unchallenged and unchanged within the school's culture and environment.

People in Manitoba were divided over the bill primarily because it sanctioned GSAs in schools. Thus, Steinbach became a flashpoint of the debate. Twelve hundred opponents of the bill in Steinbach attended a public protest meeting to voice their opposition. Ray Duerksen, the pastor of a large Steinbach church, warned city leaders, teachers, and members of the community that God could "replace them" if they did not raise their voices to oppose *Bill 18*.[3]

The principal of Steinbach Christian High School, Scott Wiebe, criticized what he saw as the bill's infringement on religious freedom.[4] According to Wiebe, "When parents and students choose an independent, faith-based school they do so specifically because it offers a certain school environment and set of values. Bill 18 erodes that choice by requiring these schools to accommodate and promote groups whose beliefs are in direct contradiction to the teachings of many independent faith-based schools."[5] Pastor Duerksen went on to condemn *Bill 18* as "the beginning of an incremental attempt to destroy the Christian church."

These are blatant examples of religion being used to undermine the right to equality for all students, including 2SLGBTQ+ students. But these schools receive 50 percent of their funding from the provincial government, and publicly funded institutions, whether in part or in full, cannot be permitted – and have no right – to implement rules or policies that interfere with the legitimate interests of *all* students.

For Evan Wiens, the issue was personal. As the only openly gay student at his school, Evan wanted to start a GSA. He told the *Globe and*

Mail that he never expected to wage a battle or become embroiled in a province-wide debate that subsequently garnered national attention.[6] "I've gone through a lot of hard times," he said, "but I've grown as a person. I want them to know that it's not a bad thing to be yourself, and you don't have to be ashamed to walk down the hallway and say, 'Hey, this is who I am.'"

The principal of Evan's school gave him permission to start a GSA. But the principal giveth and the principal taketh away – in an act that was clearly not "accommodating" 2SLGBTQ+ students, he prohibited Evan from putting up posters in the school to promote the group.[7] *Bill 18* had not yet become law in Manitoba, but when it did, Evan's principal would be compelled to allow the posters.

Evan's argument is both unassuming and personal. He has also expressed a clear-eyed view of the current state of the law. Simply put, this conflict comes down to balancing the safety of 2SLGBTQ+ students against largely perceived but completely unsubstantiated, insignificant infringements on religious freedoms.

What then is the content and scope of freedom of religion?

FREEDOM OF RELIGION

As more and more schools mandate GSAs in an effort to change school climates, the opposing argument that inevitably crops up is that such a proposal would interfere with freedoms protected by the *Charter*. So what does the *Charter* protect, and are there limits to the scope of that protection?

Section s 2(a) of the *Charter* states:

> Everyone has the following fundamental freedoms: (a) freedom of conscience and religion.[8]

Both religion and sexuality are protected by the equality guarantees in section 15 of the *Charter*:

> Every individual is equal before and under the law and has the right to the equal protection and equal benefit of the law without discrimination and, in particular, without discrimination based

on race, national or ethnic origin, colour, religion, sex, age or mental or physical disability.

Although section 15 makes no explicit reference to sexuality, in 1995's *Egan v Canada*,[9] the Supreme Court of Canada decided that protection on the basis of sexual orientation could be inferred in the provision – or, in legal terms, "read in."

Schools are governed by both the *Charter* and human rights legislation. Provincial, territorial, and federal human rights legislation also offers protection based on sexual orientation and religion when dealing with employers or landlords,[10] or others who provide services to the public. This protection reinforces the basic principle that one should not be treated with less dignity and/or respect simply because of one's sexuality or religious beliefs.

The *Saskatchewan Human Rights Code, 2018*, for instance, states in s. 13(1) that "[e]very person and every class of persons shall enjoy the right to education in any school ... without discrimination on the basis of a prohibited ground other than age."[11] Religion, sexual orientation, and gender identity are covered in this provision as prohibited grounds.[12]

The principle that freedom of religion provides an individual with the right to hold religious beliefs of their own choosing is well-established.[13] But what is the scope of religious protection in the context of public education?

A number of cases have gone to the Supreme Court of Canada to test the limits of this. The Supreme Court of Canada stated this right in general terms:

> The essence of the concept of religion is the right to entertain such religious beliefs as a person chooses, the right to declare religious beliefs openly and without fear of hindrance or reprisal, and the right to manifest belief by worship and practice or by teaching and dissemination.[14]

But the right to *hold* a belief is, as stated by the Supreme Court of Canada, broader than the right to *act* on that belief.[15] Beliefs and actions are not the same thing. This was the argument that Donn

Short had tried to make before the Winnipeg Legislature in relation to *Bill 18*.

Protecting 2SLGBTQ+ human rights was not impacting anyone's religious beliefs.

On the other hand, the attempt to prohibit GSAs in schools *was* impacting the rights of 2SLGBTQ+ students.

Many people feel that even acknowledging the rights of 2SLGBTQ+ students infringes upon freedom of religion. But the purpose of *Charter* protection is to safeguard against the government taking steps to infringe upon the freedom to hold and express religious beliefs – and to engage in religious practices derived from religious beliefs.

From the beginning, the Supreme Court of Canada qualified freedom of religion, accepting that freedom of religion must not refute the rights and freedoms of others.[16] For those seeking social justice for 2SLGBTQ+ students and for the students themselves, a few cases are pivotal in establishing the growing legal protection for 2SLGBTQ+ students, pointing the way forward for 2SLGBTQ+ and their allies as they face unfamiliar challenges – or old arguments being asserted without this important understanding of the law's support.

The only absolute truth about rights is that rights are not absolute.

The fact that freedom of religion is not an absolute right is one of the most misunderstood aspects of that right. In the United States, this same misunderstanding of the law can be seen in protests from gun owners who regard their right to bear arms as sacrosanct.

• • • • • • •

KEY CASE
Trinity Western University v British Columbia College of Teachers
2001 SCC 31

The Supreme Court of Canada distinguished between the right to hold a religious belief and the right to act on that belief, with the freedom to hold beliefs being broader than the freedom to act on them. Tolerance of different beliefs is a hallmark of a democratic society. Acting on those beliefs, however, is a very different matter.

• •

But rights are not sacrosanct. Nor are they immune to qualification or limitation to ensure and protect the rights of others.

This basic fact is likely to be a surprise to many, particularly those asserting their rights. But the Supreme Court of Canada has stated the principle clearly:[17]

> *Charter* rights are not absolute ... Application of *Charter* values must take into account other interests and in particular other *Charter* values which may conflict with their unrestricted and literal enforcement.

Another related principle in understanding the rights protected by the *Charter* is that there is no ascending or descending hierarchy of rights. This means, simply, that your right is no more important, nor is it less important, than mine.

This, too, is a value resoundingly championed by the Supreme Court time and again:[18]

> A hierarchical approach to rights, which places some [rights] over others, must be avoided, both when interpreting the *Charter* and when developing the common law. When the protected rights of two individuals come into conflict, as can occur ... *Charter* principles require a balance to be achieved that fully respects the importance of both sets of rights.

● ● ● ● ● ● ● ● ● ● ● ● ● ● ● ● ● ● ●

RIGHTS ARE NOT ABSOLUTE

Freedom of religion is not absolute.

There is no hierarchy of *Charter* rights in which one right is more important than another. When freedom of religion conflicts with the rights of 2SLGBTQ+ students, both sets of rights must be balanced and respected.

● ●

SEXUAL ORIENTATION EQUALITY RIGHTS

Freedom from discrimination based on sexual orientation is also protected by the *Charter*. This protection, however, was not originally articulated in the *Charter*. The equality rights safeguards, ensuring equal protection and benefits of the law, are found in section 15(1) of the *Charter*, which states:

> Every individual is equal before and under the law and has the right to the equal protection and equal benefit of the law without discrimination and, *in particular*, without discrimination based on race, national or ethnic origin, colour, religion, sex, age or mental or physical disability.

The use of the words "in particular" have been interpreted by the courts as meaning that the list of protected grounds following those words was not closed or exhaustive. In other words, the very language of section 15(1) leaves the door open for the later inclusion of other groups of people.

In time, and with little difficulty, the Supreme Court of Canada concluded that the law should also prohibit discrimination based upon sexual orientation.[19] Therefore, while "sexual orientation" does not actually appear in the list, those words are "read in" by courts to be included. Therefore, the equality provisions of section 15(1) apply to 2SLGBTQ+ persons as much as they apply to any other group specifically enumerated there.

Just as the Supreme Court of Canada read in sexual orientation to the *Charter*, the court also ordered that sexual orientation be read in to the Alberta human rights statute, which for many years did not include it.[20] Today, all provincial and territorial human rights legislation includes sexual orientation by name.

Therefore, the protection afforded 2SLGBTQ+ persons is complete at law. The *Charter* protects 2SLGBTQ+ persons, including students, from discriminatory treatment by the government, and human rights legislation extends protection to 2SLGBTQ+ persons from discriminatory treatment in housing, employment, and schools.

The Supreme Court of Canada, therefore, has made it clear that while freedom of religion is subject to protection by the *Charter*, so, too, are the equality rights of 2SLGBTQ+ persons.[21] In order to establish that religious freedom has been infringed upon then there must be evidence of a "significant infringement" to that belief as a result of state action.

COMPETING RIGHTS

When two people assert rights that conflict, the courts try to accommodate both rights claims; however, as rights claims based on sexuality on one hand and freedom of religion on the other become more complex, adversarial, and even aggressive, administrators of schools, legislators, and the courts have struggled to find a way to balance said competing claims.

These conflicts often begin with the assertion of a rights claim based upon the equality rights of 2SLGBTQ+ persons and a subsequent complaint based on freedom of religion. What does it mean to claim that religion-based rights have been infringed or encroached upon?

Since "reading in" sexual orientation into the *Charter* in 1995, the Supreme Court of Canada has rejected claims derived from mere feelings that one's rights have been infringed.

The court has shaped and restricted what constitutes an infringement of freedom of religion. As the legal characterization of equality rights based on sexual orientation has become more detailed, it has, arguably, also become more difficult to prevail on religion-based claims. This is certainly true when the thrust of a complaint is from those who would rather not acknowledge the equality rights of 2SLGBTQ+ students. This attitude was, in fact, quite common in the public protests around *Bill 18* in Manitoba and a similar bill, *Bill 13*, also known as the *Accepting Schools Act*, in Ontario.[22] And that is all it was – an attitude. But feeling this way does not amount to an infringement on one's freedom of religion.

Constructing safe schools for 2SLGBTQ+ students ensures that these students have access to education the way all other students do. Permitting students to form a GSA, and even obliging a school to establish such a group when requested by students, has no impact on the belief systems of other students, their parents, or anyone else.

The same argument was made in relation to same-sex marriage. There, it was claimed that mere permission being extended to same-sex persons to marry offended religious freedoms. But the argument was as misguided then as it is now.

The Supreme Court of Canada made it very clear that "the mere recognition of the equality rights of one group" – 2SLGBTQ+ students for instance – "cannot, in itself, constitute a violation" of the equality rights of another, say for example, those asserting religious freedom rights.[23] Importantly, the court went on to observe that "the promotion of *Charter* rights and values enriches our society as a whole and the furtherance of those rights cannot undermine the very principles the *Charter* was meant to foster."[24]

FREEDOM OF RELIGION – WHAT DOES IT *NOT* LOOK LIKE?

To understand what infringes on a religious belief, it is first necessary to understand what constitutes a religious belief. One such case is particularly relevant. *Syndicat Northcrest v Amselem*, considered by the Supreme Court of Canada in 2004, is essential to understanding how the law offers support to 2SLGBTQ+ students in the face of religious objections.[25]

The facts of *Amselem* were pretty straightforward. In September 1996, to celebrate the Jewish week-long festival of Sukkot, Mr. Amselem and others constructed a "succah," a decorated hut, on each of the balconies of their Place Northcrest apartments. The board, Syndicat Northcrest, requested that the succahs be removed in accordance with the building's bylaws.

A year later, Mr. Amselem requested permission to set up a succah on his balcony and the Syndicat said no. Syndicat Northcrest offered to permit residents to construct a communal succah in the gardens of the building, but Mr. Amselem and other Jewish residents declined the proposed accommodation. They asserted that their beliefs required them to construct a succah on each person's own balcony.

In response, Syndicat Northcrest filed an application for an injunction prohibiting the appellants from setting up succahs on their balconies, and allowing for the removal or destruction of the succahs if the residents did not comply.

The case made its way to the Supreme Court of Canada to decide a number of issues, including whether or not the clauses in the bylaws infringed on the rights to freedom of religion enjoyed by Mr. Amselem and the other Jewish residents. The court also looked at whether or not Mr. Amselem and the other residents had waived their rights to freedom of religion when they moved in, by agreeing to abide by the existing bylaws.

The Supreme Court set out a two-stage process or test for establishing if something is an infringement of freedom of religion under the *Charter*. The first step is for someone alleging a violation of religious beliefs or practices to show that they have a sincerely held belief related to religion.

The court has made clear that it is the "sincerely held belief" that is subject to *Charter* protection. There is no requirement on a person asserting the protection of the *Charter* to establish that their belief is a mandatory part of religious doctrine or required religious practice.

A religious belief is simply a sincere belief that someone holds in order to connect with the divine.[26] It is not necessary that all followers of a particular religion share each and every belief. This means that the test of whether or not someone holds a sincere, religious belief – which is subject to legal protection – is purely subjective. The courts are prepared to accept an individual's beliefs as worthy of protection, and to give said beliefs very broad recognition.

• • • • • • •

KEY CASE
Syndicat Northcrest v Amselem
2004 SCC 47

Freedom of religion consists of the freedom for an individual to undertake practices and hold beliefs related to a specific religion, demonstrating what they sincerely believe or are undertaking in order to connect with the divine or as a practice of their spiritual faith, regardless of whether or not a particular practice or belief is required by official religious dogma or is in conformity with the position of religious officials.

While the court will resist ruling on the validity of a religious belief or practice, if the belief is in dispute, the court will investigate the sincerity of a belief if sincerity is at issue.[27] Once someone has demonstrated that their religious freedom has been engaged, the court must then determine whether or not there has been *sufficient* interference to constitute an infringement of freedom of religion.

While the establishment of a sincerely held religious belief is largely a subjective test, when it comes to establishing infringement on a claimant's religious freedoms, the Supreme Court stressed the need for objective evidence of a violation.[28] In other words, religious belief is subjective and personal, and may vary from one individual to the next, even among worshippers from the same religion. Sincere religious belief is deeply felt and of profound importance to people of faith; however, when it is alleged that religious freedoms have been infringed, the courts will ask for more than a personal affront – they will ask if there is external evidence that a reasonable person would consider, and then agree with, in pointing to a violation of said sincere belief.

The court made clear in *Amselem* that section 2(a) of the *Charter* "prohibits only burdens or impositions on religious practice that are non-trivial," going on to say:[29]

> It consequently suffices that a claimant show that the impugned contractual or legislative provision (or conduct) interferes with his or her ability to act in accordance with his or her religious beliefs in a manner that is more than trivial or insubstantial.

This is an important point for several reasons. Chief among them, that many people (including teachers, administrators, parents, and students) may not realize that freedom of religion is not absolute.

It is insufficient to argue that a person's religious freedoms have been interfered with or, in legal terms, infringed when confronted by 2SLGBTQ+ students, teachers, or allies seeking to establish programs, policies, or student groups that support the rights of 2SLGBTQ+ students and staff. Only burdens to some significant degree are considered problematic.

While there may be some question as to "how much" infringement will be allowed, when it comes to arguments against 2SLGBTQ+ rights and claims that freedom of religion is being threatened, some infringement is permissible.

NEW ATTITUDE

Laws that permit students to form a GSA have no impact on the belief systems of other students, their parents, a school division, or anyone else. *Bill 18* does not impose religious beliefs on anyone.

The Supreme Court of Canada has stated clearly that merely recognizing the equality rights of one group – sexual and gender minority students in this instance – does not in itself constitute an infringement on the equality rights of another,[30] such as those asserting religious freedom rights. As such, *Bill 18* did not violate guaranteed freedoms.

At most, any interference that could possibly be pointed to as a result of allowing a GSA to thrive in any school would be trivial. And what would constitute an infringement? Requiring an administrative assistant to make a room booking or photocopying posters or dealing with other minor administrative matters related to the GSA? These are all less than trivial.

Evan Wiens decided to fight for other gay students who were too fearful to speak for themselves. But in doing so, he tackled powerful voices who opposed him, including Manitoba Conservative MP Vic Toews, federal minister for public safety, who relied upon arguments grounded in freedom of religion. In a letter to his constituents, Toews termed the bill an "unconstitutional infringement upon the freedom of religion." This is an old and inaccurate argument, calling for new thinking based on an understanding of what the law actually says.

The objective of measures taken in schools by teachers and administration, and the students themselves, is almost always – like *Bill 18* itself – to ensure that all students, including those who are 2SLGBTQ+, have safe and equal access to education. Given these benefits, it is difficult to see how any argument that pits the legal protections of 2SLGBTQ+ students against religious freedom – either of students, teachers, or of an entire school division – could be anything other than weak and would, in our view, have to give way to an equality rights claim by or on behalf of students.

> **KEY CASE**
> **R v Big M Drug Mart Ltd**
> **[1985] 1 SCR 295**
>
> *Freedom of Religion*
> Includes the right to hold religious beliefs, to declare those beliefs openly, and to put those beliefs into practice through worship, teaching, and dissemination.
>
> *Limitations*
> Freedom of religion is not absolute and can be limited to protect public safety, health, or, significantly, the rights and freedoms of others.

Freedom of religion includes the right to engage in religious practices and to declare one's religious beliefs openly. Some will argue that they are compelled by religious belief to speak out against 2SLGBTQ+ students and the presence of GSAs in schools. But speaking out against 2SLGBTQ+ students and the mere presence of GSAs is, in a word, hateful. For some, speaking out means going beyond attitude and beliefs to employing hateful and discriminatory language. It is well-established, however, that religious freedoms are subject to limitations necessary for protecting the safety and/or fundamental rights and freedoms of others.

The same is true for freedom of expression. Arguments against 2SLGBTQ+ students and persons are often grounded in freedom of religion as well as freedom of expression. For example, there is the case of Bill Whatcott, who wanted to make homosexuality illegal.

Under the name of "Christian Truth Activists," Bill Whatcott placed flyers in mailboxes at homes in Saskatoon and Regina in 2001 and 2002. Four people who received the flyers filed complaints with the Saskatchewan Human Rights Commission on the basis that the flyers promoted "hatred against individuals because of their sexual orientation."

Whatcott also protested at gay pride events, and in 2001, he held a Heterosexual Pride Day in Regina.

In 2005, he was fined $17,500 by the Saskatchewan Human Rights Tribunal for distributing material deemed hateful toward gay people. Whatcott appealed the fine through every court in Saskatchewan, eventually taking his case to the Supreme Court of Canada.

In February 2013, the Supreme Court of Canada ruled that freedom of religious speech and the freedom to teach or share religious beliefs was subject to reasonable limitations.[31] In particular, the court said religious freedom is limited by the requirement that the exercising of these rights not be accomplished through hate speech.

If others like Whatcott believed they had free rein to say whatever they wanted about 2SLGBTQ+ people as part of their right to free expression and freedom of religion, this decision made clear that any such "understanding" of their rights was mistaken.

* * *

"KEEP HOMOSEXUALITY OUT OF SASKATOON'S PUBLIC SCHOOLS!"
Flyer distributed by Bill Whatcott in Saskatchewan

It has come to the attention of the Christian Truth Activists that a committee on "Gay, Lesbian, Bisexual and Transgendered issues," set up by the Saskatoon Public School Board had recommended that information on homosexuality be included in their curriculum and school libraries. The elementary school teacher's union in Ontario voted this year in favour of this for grades 3 and 4, even though children at this age are more interested in playing Barbie & Ken rather than learning how wonderful it is for two men to sodomize each other.

Children in Ontario perform poorly in terms of academics; however, their teachers seem more interested in sexual politics of a perverted type, rather than preparing children to do well when they are older. Now the homosexuals want to share their filth and propaganda with Saskatchewan's children. They did it in Boston, under the guise of "Safe Schools" and their little sensitivity class degenerated into a filthy session where gay and lesbian teachers used dirty language to describe lesbian sex and sodomy in their teenage audience.

* * *

HATE SPEECH

Hate speech is speech that rises beyond causing emotional distress to individual members of a specific group, potentially leading to wider societal impact. The Supreme Court of Canada recognized in *Whatcott* that if a group of people are considered inferior, subhuman, or lawless, it is easier to justify denying said group and its members' equal rights or status.

Resulting from *Whatcott*, the Supreme Court made clear that hate speech was not protected speech in the public arena. Rules against offensive expression can be even stronger in a closed environment like a school or workplace. In schools, as is the case for employees in places of employment, students have the right to be free from harassment, belittlement, and ridicule.

Attempts to delegitimize and marginalize 2SLGBTQ+ students are commonplace in schools, some more than others, and is often the norm.[32]

In schools, therefore, it is even clearer that any speech that delegitimizes and rejects a particular group in the eyes of the majority should not be permitted. It is in that same context that the opposition to *Bill 18* unfolded in Manitoba, a space populated by vulnerable teenagers.

Rather than undermining *Bill 18*, as many argued at the time, Canadian law establishes that *Bill 18* was built on solid legal ground, and achieved a just and appropriate balance between the rights of both sides engaged by the legislation.

Bill 18 took direct aim at homophobic language and conduct by naming it, and by providing every-corner-of-every-school affirmation and recognition that 2SLGBTQ+ rights are human rights, and that hateful speech and conduct would not be condoned. *Bill 18* promoted gender equity, antiracism, and respect for people of all sexual orientations and gender identities.

Given the goals of *Bill 18* – confronting the problem of homophobic, transphobic, and gender-based bullying, and declaring the

●●●●●●●

KEY CASE

Saskatchewan (Human Rights Commission) v Whatcott
2013 SCC 11

The Supreme Court of Canada ruled that a publication or speech that exposes or tends to expose 2SLGBTQ+ persons to hatred is not permitted. Both freedom of religion and freedom of expression are limited by the requirement that neither right includes the right to engage in hate speech.

●●●●●●●●●●●●●●●●●●●●●●●●●●●●●●●●●●

human rights of all 2SLGBTQ+ students – any limitation on expression grounded in a sincerely held religious belief or discriminatory belief of any kind would almost certainly be viewed as a reasonable limitation on religious expression – even in a religion-based school.

This is the fundamental basis for what legal challenges may lie ahead.

THE ROAD LESS TRAVELLED

Canada has many religion-based schools. In some provinces, these schools have a constitutional basis to exist as religious schools.[33] Private or independent religious schools can be especially challenging when it comes to accommodating the needs and interests of 2SLGBTQ+ students. The approaches and policies these institutions take are often problematic.

Since constitutionally protected denominational schools are funded out of the public purse, it is especially objectionable that these institutions continue to hold views and policies that are inimical to the equality rights and interests of 2SLGBTQ+ students.

If these schools wish to continue to count on public funding, they must adjust their policies to avoid continued discrimination on the basis of gender identity and sexual orientation. This funding may also account, in part, for the noticeable lack of legal challenges to *Bill 18* in Manitoba.[34]

More recently, in 2018, the Supreme Court of Canada dealt with the issue of Trinity Western University's desire to establish a law school in

British Columbia.³⁵ The evangelical Christian university lost its legal battle over accreditation for a planned new law school. At the heart of the dispute was Trinity Western's insistence that new students and faculty sign and endorse a mandatory covenant that would have bound students to a strict code of conduct including abstinence from sex outside of heterosexual marriage. But law schools are regulated by provincial law societies, which have a mandate to facilitate inclusion. The Law Society of British Columbia declined to accredit Trinity Western's proposed law school because of the discriminatory nature of the covenant.

The Supreme Court agreed with the Law Society of British Columbia's decision, deciding that the covenant would deter 2SLGBTQ+ students from attending Trinity Western's law school and would put those who did attend at risk of significant harm.

While the competing rights scenario in that case took place in a university setting, whenever the courts deal with clashes of rights between 2SLGBTQ+ persons and those asserting freedom of religion, the decision has personal and cultural significance for 2SLGBTQ+ students and their allies.

Before the case arrived at the Supreme Court, the trial level judge said:

> Eliminating inequitable barriers to legal education, and thereby, to membership in the legal profession, also promotes the competence of the bar and improves the quality of legal services available to the public.
>
> As well, the Law Society was entitled to interpret the public interest in the administration of justice as being furthered by promoting diversity in the legal profession – or, more accurately, by avoiding the imposition of additional impediments to diversity in the profession in the form of inequitable barriers to entry.

In other words, the education system should be held to at least as high a standard as a law society that regulates the legal profession.

By the same token, one cannot compel personal acceptance, belief in inclusion, and celebration of sexual diversity. Until a change of the head is accompanied by a change of heart, challenges will continue to remain for 2SLGBTQ+ students in private religious schools.

The legal requirement for schools to create GSAs will not solve these problems, but they are often the first step; however, if a school is hostile toward the establishment of such a club or merely tolerates both the club and its student members, what kind of message does this send to 2SLGBTQ+ students? Just as the mere fact that the law is always changing, has changed in the past, and has great social meaning and impact, so too it is meaningful for students to have the open and public support of their teachers and, crucially, the administration. Critically, teachers and other school staff need to know that the administration supports their work toward 2SLGBTQ+ education and inclusion.[36]

DETOUR AHEAD

Before inclusive policies can be established, basic education and awareness must first take place.

Particular challenges exist for public schools in rural areas lacking support and resources for 2SLGBTQ+ students. For example, in the context of GSAs in smaller settings in Saskatchewan, it has been reported that "[r]ural areas have a unique set of struggles ... There is a lack of knowledge and awareness of what a GSA is and what its purpose is."[37]

The Ontario Catholic School Trustees' Association released *"Respecting Difference": A Resource for Catholic Schools in the Province of Ontario (Regarding the Establishment and Running of Activities or Organizations Promoting Equity and Respect for All Students)*.[38] This document was produced as a response to *Bill 13* – Ontario's version of Manitoba's *Bill 18*. *"Respecting Difference"* was to provide guidelines to Catholic school boards to help them establish "student-led organizations and activities in Catholic schools" related to equity and inclusive education policies.

In reality, the document was intended to make the argument, absent any evidence in support of its effectiveness, that "we don't need GSAs, we have this."[39] The title *"Respecting Difference"* referred to the "Catechism of the Catholic Church" (1997) as the "primary teaching document of the Church," referring to homosexual acts being "intrinsically disordered" and "contrary to the natural law." It told readers that same-sex relationships "do not proceed from a genuine affective and sexual complementarity," and that "under no circumstances can they be approved ..."[40]

It is important to note, however, that both the Ontario Catholic teachers and OECTA were very vocal in their support of *Bill 13* and 2SLGBTQ+ equality and inclusion in all schools.

As a general rule, 2SLGBTQ+ students are not accommodated in publicly-funded denominational schools because policies and laws allow for official and legislated discrimination against them.

Modest changes have occurred only because of court challenges and legislated responses.

NEW RIDERS ON THE ROAD

Transgender students are a vital part of the growing wave of those making new legal claims in Canadian schools.

Tracey Wilson, an eleven-year-old transgender girl, filed a complaint with BC's human rights commission when the private Catholic school she attended in Vancouver refused to accommodate her.[41] Wilson's family moved Tracey and her siblings to the public school system. Eventually the complaint against Tracey's former school board, the Catholic Independent Schools of the Vancouver Archdiocese, was resolved and a new policy established.

But students like Tracey should not have to transfer schools to find support and recognition.

In a policy released in July 2014, the board agreed that schools would accommodate students' needs on a case-by-case basis. That is what human rights law demands – accommodation must be individualized to take into account someone's individual situation. But the policy is significantly lacking – 2SLGBTQ+ kids deserve new, not grudgingly revised, policies to ensure their safety and well-being.

Students and their families can now formally request to be accommodated. A case management team consisting of doctors, teachers, and a pastor will agree upon a plan for each student and allow for a student's chosen name, gender pronoun, and uniform. But the policy also stresses a component of Catholic teaching that states people cannot change their gender identity, and that a school cannot support or accommodate a student who identifies as a different gender or wants to transition from one gender to another.

According to the board's superintendent, Doug Lauson, "the policy strikes an appropriate balance between meeting the needs of students and respecting the school board's religious teachings. 'We are people of the Catholic faith. Schools will be as inclusive as we can while still retaining our Catholic identity.'"[42]

Put in its best light, this is minimal and begrudging accommodation for 2SLGBTQ+ students. At its worst, it fails to recognize the inherent worth and dignity of transgender students. Moreover, it is dispiriting to note that the policy was adopted under threat of a complaint from the province's human rights commission. Had Tracey and her family not stepped forward, it is unlikely that anything would have changed at all. Ideally, the board itself should undertake the "new" rather than waiting to be pushed reluctantly into it. On the other hand, the board has made a change. Lawyer barbara findlay claimed that "[t]his is, as far as we know, certainly a North American first and probably a world first." She also indicated that it may be used elsewhere: "Not only is it important for the students in Vancouver who go to Catholic schools, but it will serve as a template for other Catholic school districts everywhere."[43]

However, there is hope for the day when the smallness of this step is regarded as just that, a small step of a much larger journey.

The Evangelical Foundation of Canada, the religious organization associated with the Steinbach Christian High School (SCHS), makes the following declaratory principles concerning sexuality:

> All people are created in the image of God and have inherent worth and value. As Christians we celebrate God's intention in creation, that sexual intimacy be reserved for the exclusive, life-long commitment of marriage, between one man and one woman. Recognizing humanity's brokenness, we affirm the need for all people to engage in the journey towards wholeness in Christ including those dealing with sexual and gender identity questions. We uphold the biblical principle to love our

neighbour and affirm that same-gender attracted people should be treated with the respect that is consistent with communicating the Good News of Jesus Christ.[44]

This statement offers a paternalistic view of sexual diversity. It suggests that those "dealing with sexual and gender identity questions" are broken or somehow deficient compared to their straight brothers and sisters. More stridently, it implies that the journey toward "wholeness" will only be complete when sexual minorities address their underlying issues with the aid of Christ.

At its most dismissive, this policy statement of principle implies that sexual minorities are morally inferior and not equal to their heterosexual counterparts – that they are in need of divine correction. The message this sends to 2SLGBTQ+ students attending SCHS is unequivocal: We will tolerate you, but we will never celebrate you for who you are because you have a moral problem that requires fixing.

Given that SCHS receives funding from the government, this perspective is troubling to say the least. The school is using religion to discount, undermine, and ignore rights grounded in sexual orientation when they run afoul of church doctrine.

Schools in Canada require policies that help all students reach their full potential as citizens – and as they themselves conceptualize their potential. During the journey to self-discovery, and while figuring out what commitments they owe to others, students will develop an identity shaped by key markers including sexuality and beliefs, which can of course include religious beliefs. This "working out" of identity is influenced by the need to become and the need to belong.

Policies must, therefore, continue to evolve while enabling practices and attitudes that permit and encourage 2SLGBTQ+ students to find and celebrate full citizenship within their schools. Policy challenges remain for all schools. This is especially true for denominational and private schools[45] since hope for full citizenship for 2SLGBTQ+ students, despite the laws and legislation that guarantee it, tends to fall on the shoulders of allies and enlightened teachers doing good work. More often than not, however, they lack the necessary support structures in place to assist them.[46]

Schools, school boards, and ministries must respond to messages that are harmful to 2SLGBTQ+ students by reconceptualizing student safety with respect to diversity, caring, inclusion, and celebration. Alongside policy makers and all those acting on behalf of these institutional actors, including teachers and administrators, they must also promote policies and engage in practices that respect the laws of general application whether at a provincial, federal, or even international level.[47]

Laws can be seen as crystallized policy statements. This is especially true in the area of human rights laws, which are aspirational in nature and reflect our deepest values and commitments about what it means to be human.

Human rights laws reflect society's beliefs as to how we should treat one another. This is particularly true in relation to people from minority groups and those who are vulnerable. It means, for example, that students who hold particular religious beliefs (or no religious beliefs at all) should not be persecuted or be made to suffer simply because of what they believe. They deserve respect. Likewise, 2SLGBTQ+ students must be protected from policies and practices that intentionally or unintentionally discriminate against them solely on the basis of their sexuality and/or identity.

School boards typically articulate policy to address how all students are treated. Those policies must not ignore, and must include, 2SLGBTQ+ students. They must also include students for whom religion plays an important part in their life.

Such policies would reflect foundational values applicable to everybody in a school's community. For example, Regina Public Schools (RPS) in Saskatchewan articulates its mission statement in the following foundational terms: "To instill the value of knowledge, the dignity of effort and the worth of the individual."[48]

RPS sets out four categories of shared values that are expressed through the form of empowering "I" statements. They are: "I belong," "I want to know," "I respect," and "I am responsible." The Division notes that these statements of shared values are intended "to support current practices, and to provide direction for the future."

For 2SLGBTQ+ students, these shared values have particular resonance. These students need to know that they belong to a school's community and can take their rightful place there and be valued. This last point is especially important as 2SLGBTQ+ people have long been subject to a unique form of marginalization: invisibility.

Ignoring these students is another form of queerphobia. It must be remembered that other minority groups in schools may also be ignored by the school; however, the difference is that when these students go home, they are most likely returning to a family that looks like them or shares their minority status.

That is unlikely for most 2SLGBTQ+ students who, in fact, often have to conceal their minority status from family members or risk rejection. While statistics show that roughly 5–10 percent of the general population identify as 2SLGBTQ+, the estimated proportion of homeless youth in Canada is 25–40 percent.[49] Thus, 2SLGBTQ+ youth face discrimination at home, at school, and also in the shelter system.

NEW REALITIES, CHANGING TIMES

The reality that GSAs in schools are beneficial cannot be doubted – or denied – anymore.[50]

The fact that homophobia and transphobia still thrive in Canadian schools is disturbing, but not surprising. Homophobic language and harassment are still viewed as a normal part of growing up by many people. Transphobia is real.

The heartbreaking case of fifteen-year-old Jamie Hubley, a gay student, underscores the most tragic outcome of homophobia.

Jamie Hubley died by suicide in October 2011, before Ontario extended legal protection to students requesting the creation of a GSA in their schools. Jamie, who was in Grade 10 at A.Y. Jackson High School in Ottawa, blogged about the despair and isolation he felt as a gay student. His family said that Jamie had told them he had been called vicious names in the hallways at school.

Underscoring the need to also address cyberbullying – off school activities that impact students and are constructed by school life – Jamie was harassed online after he tried to set up a GSA at his school. As is often the case, the resistance to the GSA came not only from students but also the administration – Jamie's attempts to establish a GSA were thwarted by school officials who refused to allow a school club so named. The most the school would agree to was the moniker "Rainbow Alliance."

That situation has since changed in Ontario and the law now requires school boards and school administrators to agree to what Jamie Hubley had sought – for himself and for other 2SLGBTQ+ students.

In Manitoba, Evan Wiens successfully established Steinbach Regional Secondary School's first GSA – and posters were allowed. Many people supported and applauded Evan, and he later served as Honorary Grand Marshal of Winnipeg's Pride Parade. A year after his very public efforts to have 2SLGBTQ+ students accommodated in his school, in recognition of his commitment to his community, TD Bank Group selected Evan to receive a $70,000 TD Scholarship for Community Leadership.[51]

Afterwards, Evan acknowledged there was a backlash against him in his school, but said the negatives were outweighed by the positive support he received.[52] He even received a lot of support from religious communities – a thing very true to the new realities developing within schools.

As is frequently the case with polarizing issues, contradictory propositions often exist. Some religious persons remain opposed to 2SLGBTQ+ rights, while others support them. According to Evan, some religious leaders in the community offered private support of his efforts on behalf of 2SLGBTQ+ students as others in the city stood against him.[53]

Private support is good, but it needs to come out of the closet – publicly articulated support from religious leaders would hold sway over the thinking of many adherents.

EVAN WIENS, STUDENT ACTIVIST

"I know there are a few churches in Steinbach that do support gay rights and do support same-sex marriage within their churches, so I think for those people to come forward to start voicing their concerns … can really help push schools."

The last word goes to those who seek to defend freedom of religion – people who can be, and sometimes are, allies of 2SLGBTQ+ students.

Rev. George Feenstra of Steinbach United Church offered public support to Evan. Rev. Feenstra promoted acceptance and inclusiveness to his congregation, and urged them to live by those ideals in their day-to-day lives. "What people feel is that their faith is being attacked by the inclusion of these persons. And that's an interesting point of view because years ago there were people in the church resistant to the idea that women were full human beings."[54]

Rev. Feenstra, a member of Steinbach's Neighbours for Community, a group that included other religious leaders and which promoted acceptance and inclusion of 2SLGBTQ+ students in a city that once stood firmly against *Bill 18*, observes: "I think that the tide is shifting."[55]

2
The Safe and Welcoming School

ASK (*VERB*): TO PUT A QUESTION TO SOMEONE, OR TO REQUEST AN ANSWER FROM SOMEONE

Gabriel Picard asked a simple question: *Am I safe here?*

A simple question for Picard, though the question was provocative – and threatening – to others. School administrators, teachers, and officials were particularly put on edge by it.

To ensure he received an answer, Picard posed the question in the form of a legal complaint against his school and the associated school board – the Lakehead District School Board, in Thunder Bay, Ontario. He alleged that the board, in violation of sections 1 and 9 of the Ontario *Human Rights Code*, had "discriminated" against him. Since Grade 9, Picard – because of his sexual orientation – had been repeatedly harassed, causing a "poisoned and unsafe" climate for him, and the school board had failed to act. After four years, he had had enough. Picard filed a human rights complaint with the specific goal of changing the culture of his high school. He understood that re-imagining the school was the only way to ensure a safe place for himself, other 2SLGBTQ+ students and teachers.

In time, Picard's complaint resulted in a settlement with the school board that called for a number of solutions. First, the board agreed to develop and adopt a document entitled "Proactive Steps in Preventing Homophobic Harassment." The board also committed to a review of its policies, agreeing to make any necessary changes. Most important,

GABRIEL PICARD, HUMAN RIGHTS COMPLAINT

"I am gay and I believe my right to equal treatment with respect to services, goods and facilities without discrimination because of my sexual orientation has been infringed by the respondents. I believe this is contrary to ... the Human Rights Code ... I believe this [because] ... since grade nine, I have been repeatedly harassed by numerous students because of my sexual orientation ... This has caused a poisoned and unsafe environment for me in the school."

they agreed to promote curriculum resources and professional development in order to confront homophobia – and also heterosexism.

The school board committed to the establishment of a GSA and designated safe spaces in every high school in the school district. Under the agreement, a newly instituted Diversity Committee was charged with promoting additional programs and proposals in order to make district schools "safer."

Unfortunately, success on paper did not immediately translate into success on the ground. Gabriel Picard, with the assistance of his mother, Ellen Chambers Picard, a high school teacher at his former high school, brought further complaints before the Human Rights Commission in Ontario in order to compel the school board to comply with its obligations under the settlement agreement.

This is the ongoing problem with settlement agreements. They tend to be confidential, their contents unknown except between the parties involved. Who then monitors compliance?

In this case, Gabe Picard and his mother were committed to ensure the agreement was followed.

Some schools respond to bullying when it happens, but this is merely a reactive, punitive response. This is a slight improvement from the days when teasing and bullying were viewed as a normal and ignorable part of going to school.

School is the principal public setting in which 2SLGBTQ+ children and youth emerge as a vulnerable population at risk of marginalization, harassment, and violence. And yet dealing with bullying before it occurs is still a threatening idea to some. This is because proactive responses require making a connection between school culture and bullying. In many cases, this means implicating the dominant culture as being the thrust of the problem, and responding to the religious beliefs of some who oppose and are frightened by changes in a culture that, for them, has been comfortable and part of their own unchallenged identities, beliefs, and practices for most of their lives. Not all people of faith will feel challenged by this change – indeed many are supportive of 2SLGBTQ+-inclusive work. But for those who do feel threatened, they may feel that their very identities are being critiqued and brought into question.

We hope this book makes clear that the right to hold and to manifest sincerely held religious beliefs is a right deserving of respect and protection in law; however, freedom of religion is not absolute and can be limited to protect public safety, health, or, significantly, the rights and freedoms of others.

DO I HAVE A CHOICE?

Some school administrators do not want to deal with bullying at all. There are numerous reasons for this. Often, administrators have professional aspirations and do not want to be known as having come from a "problem" school. There are also hesitations about dealing with the feared angry parent – notwithstanding that many parents are supportive of the kind of proactive 2SLGBTQ+-inclusive education that we are advocating for in this book.

Teachers very often point to the political nature of the vice-principal's office as the reason anti-harassment policies are not implemented. Vice-principals may have their eye on a higher position within the school board and do not wish to deal with what are still controversial policies for some – particularly parents.

Frightened of appearing in support of same sex–attracted students (and relationships), administrators may not support specific school initiatives intended to make schools more inclusive of 2SLGBTQ+ students. A school's vice-principal may feel that they need community support before enforcing such policies.

BULLYING

Bullying is behaviour that is intended to cause, or should be known to cause, fear, intimidation, humiliation, distress or other forms of harm to another person's body, feelings, self-esteem, reputation or property; or is intended to create, or should be known to create, a negative school environment for another person.

— *The Schools Act, Manitoba*

If an administrator asks, "Do I have a choice?" the answer is no. And here's why.

Ten years before Gabriel Picard's human rights complaint in Ontario, Azmi Jubran dared to question his school's culture in British Columbia with a risky inquiry of his own. For five years, from 1993 through 1998, Azmi Jubran attended Handsworth Secondary School in North Vancouver, where he was repeatedly assaulted both verbally and physically. He was subjected to homophobic epithets, spit and urinated on, and kicked and punched by male and female students.

After defending himself during an assault of which he was the target, Jubran faced criminal charges. Though he was acquitted, as a result of his experience before a criminal court and before he graduated from high school, Jubran filed a human rights complaint before the Human Rights Tribunal in British Columbia alleging that he was discriminated against on the basis of sexual orientation – a prohibited ground.

Like Gabriel Picard, Azmi Jubran asked a straightforward question about school safety: *Does a school have an obligation to provide a safe environment for all students?* This was at the time a provocative idea. Jubran alleged that the Board of School Trustees was answerable for the discrimination he faced because the trustees failed to provide an educational environment free from harassment by failing to respond effectively to discriminatory conduct.

●●●●●●●

KEY CASE
North Vancouver School District No 44 v Jubran
(British Columbia Court of Appeal)
2005 BCCA 201

The fact that Azmi Jubran was not gay was irrelevant. The effect of the homophobic bullying to which he was subjected was the same whether or not Jubran's victimizers perceived him correctly. Homophobic harassment ascribed to Jubran the negative perceptions, myths, and stereotypes attributed to gay students.

●●●●●●●●●●●●●●●●●●●●●●●●●●●●●●●●●●

Azmi Jubran identified as heterosexual. Heterosexual students are often subjected to homophobic harassment and/or feel distress at the harassment of 2SLGBTQ+ students.[1]

Bullying of any kind is based upon a desire to vilify difference. Bullying establishes the victimizer as a member of a privileged class – what is perceived as normal, dominant, or desirable. The actual identity of the victimized can be less important than the statement such harassment makes about the victimizer. Harassing someone for being "gay" makes a public statement to peers that the victimizer is not what they condemn.

Some people made an ill-advised argument that because Azmi Jubran was not gay, he could not claim the protection of the Human Rights Code on the basis of sexual orientation. But the Human Rights Tribunal found Jubran's own sexual orientation to be irrelevant in the matter at hand. Whether someone is or perceived (correctly or incorrectly) to be 2SLGBTQ+ is not even a question that should be asked. The question is whether or not the harassment is grounded in prejudice against a particular sexual orientation.

No credit to itself, the school board appealed the decision to the British Columbia Supreme Court, and that court in turn decided that Jubran, because he was heterosexual, had not been discriminated against.

The basis upon which these decisions were being argued seems, hopefully, characteristic of a past that no longer exists or is at least on its way out. Unfortunately, schools are often contradictory patchworks at the best and worst of times. There are still students, parents, teachers, and administrators who cling to outdated beliefs and knowledge.

In short, lack of knowledge and/or experience is yet another driver of the need to adopt a new school – and public – culture. The law is moving along and creating a new environment for those students who benefit from and are, as is the case with both Picard and Jubran, responsible for it. But there are others who need to be brought along.

The Court of Appeal sensibly disagreed with the trial court and decided that Jubran's sexual orientation was irrelevant. What was at issue was the harassment he'd received. It was decided that school boards had an obligation to provide a safe learning environment, free from discrimination. Period.

The Supreme Court of Canada declined to hear an appeal and therefore the matter was settled. As a result, after over thirty thousand dollars in legal fees, twenty-four-year-old Azmi Jubran prevailed.

WANTING TOO MUCH

The idea of taking proactive steps to respond to a culture of bullying at schools was not settled, accepted, or even much promoted when Azmi Jubran or Gabe Picard asked their schools to do just that. They were both leaders, visionaries, heroes.

By ignoring 2SLGBTQ+ students, the existing climate of many schools marginalizes and renders them invisible. The use of offensive words to define 2SLGBTQ+ students harms them. Today, more and more schools are taking proactive steps to confront and counter these issues. We have seen this with the movement to legally protect GSAs in schools.

Gabe Picard recalled a conversation he had with the principal of his high school. He told her that hanging one "Positive Space" flag on a doorknob in the basement was not sufficient to make his experience safe in her school. When she asked him what he wanted, he told her, "I want to change the school culture. If you can't change this culture, then you've failed as an educator because that's what it's all about."

His principal replied, "No, we can't change a culture. You want too much."

IT'S NOT YOUR PARENT'S (CONCEPTION OF) SAFETY ANYMORE

According to students and teachers across Canada, there is a range of conceptions regarding safety at schools.[2] This range corresponds to the degree to which the safety concerns and needs of sexual- and gender-minority students are variously considered.

For a few schools, the conception of safety is equated with equity, inclusion, and celebration. This is a marvel for sexual-minority students. At other schools, sexual-minority students are ignored or incidentally considered only when administrations have been compelled to do so.

When security is viewed as the primary ingredient in ensuring a safe school, the emphasis in the school is on physical safety. Here, schools emphasize security measures instead of equity. At these schools, safety concerns often focus on visible-minority students, who are often perceived to be the greatest threat to a school's safety.[3]

Equity policies are secondary to concerns about immediate, often extreme violence. Frequently, discussions of safety focus exclusively on the presence of gangs in schools. Students at such schools – often students of colour – are read as dangerous, and the particular threat to be controlled almost inevitably male.

Safety, then, is equated with surveillance cameras, dress policies, security guards, and an emphasis on containing and, if unsuccessful, responding to violent behaviours. Schools that approach safety in this limited way also often attempt to control student identities via restrictive dress codes that prohibit baggy pants, hoodies, and head gear.

The process of "othering" these students pushes black students – some or all – away from the "normal" centre, as it is perceived by the policy actors creating safe school policies at these schools. Othering marginalizes and produces inequities and alienation. Teachers who create safe school policies are given enormous influence and power.

One result of such far-reaching influence is that black students in these schools often internalize the label "dangerous," which is thrust upon them, resulting in a diminished social standing within their schools. Invariably, the ultimate result of this can be a self-fulfilling prophecy – that is, the label comes to be accepted even by the students. As a result, the students then come to behave in ways the labels suggest they should.

In some schools, beyond pursuing safety as security, the administration pushes things even further and attempts to *control* the identities of their students, particularly black male students. This is all undertaken in an attempt to mitigate the threat of students perceived as potentially dangerous by socially constructing them as white.

At these schools, safety means responding to physical violence as it occurs, with preventative measures aimed at keeping weapons and unauthorized persons off of school property and monitoring students inside schools. Security guards and surveillance cameras are the norm, as are constant conversations and warnings about crime and dress codes.

The dress code at many schools forbids hats so that faces are not obscured for security cameras. Baggy pants and anything to do with hip hop culture is out. The environment at these schools is toxic, and students do not perceive safety in the same way as the school does. 2SLGBTQ+ students do not even register.

Schools like these can develop a reputation as being schools for "rejects." Anyone with academic ability – and means – transfers out. School authority is used to control students, not to make school space safer. Authentic school safety, then, is ignored.

SAFETY IGNORED

For 2SLGBTQ+ students, schools that pursue safety and see the threat to school safety at the level of the individual ignore the needs of 2SLGBTQ+ students, who are not seen as factors in any safety equation. For most sexual-minority students, an emphasis on safety, security, surveillance, and punishment does not translate into constructing a safe school. The result is a chilling experience for 2SLGBTQ+ students who must now fend for themselves.

Moreover, the result of this conception of a safe school ignores many other aspects of school life that have profound and negative effects on school culture, particularly for sexual-minority students whose concerns get shunted aside when the emphasis on keeping schools safe is on surveillance and controlling an environment, and where the focus is on physical violence – indeed, extreme violence.

To the degree that bullying is acknowledged only in generic terms, homophobic and transphobic bullying are not specifically considered. Bullying remains a general concept and is seen only as specific violent incidents occurring between and among particular students. Homophobia and transphobia in schools, as prominent forms of bullying, remain largely unacknowledged.

Incident-bound policy approaches governed by this mindset fail to acknowledge the cultural factors at play, which are critical in making schools safer and more inclusive for 2SLGBTQ+ students. The ideological implications of what is transpiring in schools and on schoolyards are missed.

Safe school intervention strategies must be based upon a more expansive perspective strategy that locates bullying in its cultural context. Approaches aimed at persuading victimizers not to victimize do nothing to change school culture, the key component in resolving the problem of bullying and oppression of sexual-minority students – to say nothing of addressing the heteronormativity of schools and school culture.

The best approaches are found in schools that promote equity as a means of achieving a safe and secure environment for students, teachers, and staff. Here the emphasis is less on schools monitoring their own students and more on not only promoting equity but actively pursuing goals of social justice. Social justice in this instance means not only the pursuit of equality but the elimination of all oppression within a given school.

For many students, heteronormativity is viewed as being more immediately threatening to their personal identities and safety than homophobic or transphobic bullying, or any fear of physical or verbal harassment or violence. To be clear, however, for students in many schools, particularly students in smaller cities and in rural settings, concerns about physical and verbal violence are still significant.

The chief ingredient of inclusion, equity, or social justice is a proactive approach in which justice is encouraged and sought out within a school's environment. This conception of safety is the ideal model for all schools, notwithstanding an acknowledgment that transformation can be a long-term goal for most schools undertaking it.

To those who might find such work wearying or, indeed, impossible, we are reminded of and point to the words of Canadian educator and scholar Peter McLaren:

> Teachers can do no better than to create agendas of possibility in their classrooms. Not every student will take part, but many will ... Some teachers may simply be unwilling to function as critical educators. Critical pedagogy does not guarantee that resistance will not take place. But it does provide teachers with the foundations for understanding resistance, so that whatever pedagogy is developed can be sensitive to sociocultural conditions ...[4]

In sum, this range of possibilities, from "security" to "control" to "equity" to "social justice," does not necessarily represent unchallengeable truths about these and other schools; rather, it is a useful means by which to view the organization of safety in educational narratives on the ground.

Many schools, no doubt, present elements of several or all of these conceptions to varying degrees. For many sexual-minority students, schools are not and have not been places of learning or even social development but places where they were abused, terrorized, and oppressed for being different.

What these conceptions establish is that oppression takes more forms than "generic" bullying. Students who are 2SLGBTQ+ perceive their safety to be threatened in ways that may differ from other students. For 2SLGBTQ+ students and their allies, the failure on the part of school administrators and others to embrace this approach is a constant reminder that their security is under threat, their safety tenuous.

THEN AND NOW

What would a new conception of safety look like?

These comments, which we have heard from teachers and students alike, capture the challenge of turning theoretical concepts into law and policy reform recommendations, and provide a useful segue to the issue of reform.

Some teachers and administrators have pointed to a reluctance in their schools to discipline students for harassment for fear of being perceived as discriminatory. Teachers understand that students pick up on this climate and take advantage of it. To what extent this occurs is difficult to say, but the point does argue in favour of a whole school approach in which the disciplinary piece is only one piece.

Teachers on the front line must feel supported. For their part, students need to know that the entire school is behind inclusive education approaches of all kinds, and that no one is being targeted – that aim is being taken at the climate and not individuals or marginalized groups.

We have heard from teachers and students themselves about how this can be accomplished. Possible reforms highlight the links between broader understandings of safety – the kind envisioned by Azmi Jubran and Gabe Picard – and the proposed reforms that students and teachers most often support.

First, there is a need for school boards, and schools, to conceptualize bullying broadly. Bullying must include not just physical violence but also verbal and attitudinal violence – and also cyberbullying and text messaging which often occur off site.

Second, there must be mandated curriculum change to reflect 2SLGBTQ+ realities and 2SLGBTQ+ lives, beginning in the early grades. Optional courses and electives will not transform a culture. Accordingly, teachers must be prepared for sexual and gender diversity education in their B.Ed. degrees, and training in policies and 2SLGBTQ+-inclusive education practices – at all times mindful of the multiple forms of oppression experienced specifically by racialized 2SLGBTQ+ students – must occur as a matter of professional development.[5]

Third, the privilege and social rank of heterosexual students must be considered. This is so because 2SLGBTQ+ content in the curriculum should not be merely "inclusive." We argue, yes, that 2SLGBTQ+ students should be included and celebrated, but leaving privilege unchallenged will not result in the necessary change in school climate.

In this broader configuration, curriculum will examine the social construction of sexuality, gender, and race for all students. The official curriculum, then, rather than sustaining the dominant order of gender and sexuality (including white privilege), will contest these cultural hierarchies. And as 2SLGBTQ+ students of colour are marginalized in multiple ways, any effort to reorganize and investigate dominant thinking must include race.

None of these proposals will matter or be realized without sufficient funding to put equity into practice. Teachers willing and, indeed, excited to do this work often complain of having a lack of resources. Administrators who are also on board bemoan inadequate budgets. To this end, there is agreement among many teachers and administrators that a well-staffed equity office at each school board is a must.

Training and professional workshops are key to providing teachers with necessary information relating to these changes. The whole school approach is relevant here as teachers who undertake a 2SLGBTQ+-inclusive education must know they have the support of the administration as well as their colleagues.

In general, both students and teachers tell us that it is necessary to begin a transformative process that will change school culture, as well as how that process needs to begin and how to sustain it when underway. Only a transformative approach will dismantle the normative powers exerted in schools, benefitting various categories of privilege.

Students and teachers also recognize that transformation on a large scale is and will be time-consuming. Which is why now is the right time to begin this process.

MOVING ON ...

The law protecting and championing 2SLGBTQ+ rights has been growing and developing in favour of said rights. That was to be expected as the recognition of 2SLGBTQ+ rights is relatively new when compared with the long-held recognition of other rights such as religious freedoms and even rights ensuring racial equality.

The position of 2SLGBTQ+ students in schools has become more secure and more celebrated. From this growing celebration in law should come strength. With that strength should come increased optimism and the determination to strive for more.

It is fair then to ask: What now? What do 2SLGBTQ+ students and their allies do *now* with their new legal sway?

For many years, concerns about the safety of 2SLGBTQ+ students often began (and ended) with discussions of physical safety, and solutions to physical and verbal harassment and bullying. More recent ideas embrace not only physical safety but define safety more broadly to include celebration and inclusion. Another word that should be thrown out on the scrap heap of history is "tolerance" – 2SLGBTQ+ students do not want to be tolerated; they want to be accepted for who they are.

These newer, broader conceptualizations of safety tackle the general climate of schools, demanding the inclusion and celebration of 2SLGBTQ+ students in approaches to school safety motivated by social justice concerns.[6]

Approaches to bullying that see bullying only in terms of specific confrontations and personal conflicts between two students have negative policy implications for the creation of the new kinds of safe, equitable, and inclusive schools being imagined by 2SLGBTQ+ students and their allies. As long as school-based efforts to combat bullying, harassment, and physical violence remain limited to strategies designed to "understand" the bully and to "contain" their actions,[7] then the needs of 2SLGBTQ+ students will continue to be ignored.

For example, when a bullied Muslim student goes home, it more likely than not means being greeted – and embraced – by Muslim parents, brothers, and sisters. It is almost never true of bullied 2SLGBTQ+ students that they are going home to 2SLGBTQ+ parents or siblings.

Narrow efforts at containment and punishment ignore how cultural factors participate in and influence conceptions of what it means for 2SLGBTQ+ students to be "safe" – and how a new kind of "safety" for 2SLGBTQ+ students can and must be achieved in schools.[8]

ON THE HOOK

The "old" conception of safety ignores many aspects of school life that have profound and negative effects on school climate.[9] This is particularly true for 2SLGBTQ+ students whose needs are not addressed when the emphasis on keeping schools safe is limited to exerting control on a few problematic students, or where the focus is on physical violence alone.[10]

Any approach that seeks to understand the bully, primarily in relation to their family background, or to locate them in an environment in which teachers and administrators fail to get involved, lets the school and the larger culture off the hook. Only with a full cultural configuration, implicating schools and the wider school climate, can the full citizenship of 2SLGBTQ+ students be achieved within safe, equitable, and inclusive schools.

Human rights law, even with its purposive approach to remedying inequalities, is an important public statement of the need to accommodate 2SLGBTQ+ students. That the official power of the state is put to this purpose sends a powerful message. But the human rights framework – in action – may not be entirely fit for that purpose.

Enforcing human rights is largely a reactive process. Only when a complaint is first brought forward can the power of the state begin to move to right a wrong. This administrative framework unfairly places a burden on students to initiate a human rights complaint when their rights are arguably infringed. For 2SLGBTQ+ students, that means "coming out" publicly when they may not be ready. The complaint process also means going up against the power and culture of the school – a daunting task for anyone.

That is why the acknowledgment that 2SLGBTQ+ rights are human rights – while important and powerful – is only a half-measure.

What can remain unaddressed in schools is a proactive approach in school governance, one that recognizes and ameliorates the day-to-day experiences of 2SLGBTQ+ students in particular schools.

Human rights law remains complaint-based, locating the onus for a legal response with the individual. A secondary problem is the signal this sends – that there is no legal obligation on behalf of the school to proactively intervene in securing equal access to education for 2SLGBTQ+ students.[11]

NEW WAYS OF SEEING

Bullying is no longer viewed as unassailable – an inevitable if unpleasant part of growing up with which all students must learn to cope. That traditional view has let parents, educators, and policy-makers off the hook. To the extent that bullying was addressed in schools, students were often told to stand up for themselves.[12] Bullying is now commonly regarded as a damaging experience in the lives of students – one that has ongoing repercussions.

Evidence demonstrates that generic policies and laws currently in effect largely guarantee that when impacted by bullying, 2SLGBTQ+ students and their complaints will be ignored[13] – if school boards, teachers, and administrators are not required to discuss issues surrounding the bullying and inclusion of 2SLGBTQ+ students, they largely will not do so. Generic safe schools and anti-bullying initiatives have not adequately considered the specific needs of 2SLGBTQ+ students.[14]

On the government of Saskatchewan's website,[15] the approach is to focus on the broad rubric of anti-bullying policies and initiatives without addressing head-on the realities of 2SLGBTQ+ students. One must dig behind the original information related to anti-bullying and go to additional links before finding information about 2SLGBTQ+ students. One link leads to a document entitled "Questions and Answers: Sexual orientation in schools."[16] The document provides clinical information and was prepared by the Public Health Agency of Canada – not even an official government of Saskatchewan document.

This approach to policy development is deeply flawed. First, the Ministry of Education does not specifically address the unique realities of 2SLGBTQ+ students. Second, the relevant information is hidden under the broader rubric of anti-bullying measures, and in any event is not readily accessible. Third, the documentation is borrowed from a third party, the government of Canada, sending the message that the government of Saskatchewan and its Ministry of Education do not take the needs of 2SLGBTQ+ students sufficiently seriously. And lastly, positioning the 2SLGBTQ+ student as a "problem" to be addressed is a continuation of old thinking that, in fact, further marginalizes 2SLGBTQ+ students.

That conception also identifies other students as "the bully" and lets the culture of the school inappropriately off the hook. Only by creating a school that includes and celebrates 2SLGBTQ+ students will all students be "safe." The school, administrators, and teachers must remain resolutely *on* the hook – with respect to the school's official educative function – to create safe schools.

2SLGBTQ+ INCLUSIVE EDUCATION

Scholars, activists, 2SLGBTQ+ students, and their allies, all committed to safe and equal schools for 2SLGBTQ+ students, argue in favour of inclusive, anti-oppressive policies and pedagogies that accommodate and celebrate diversity. These policies and curriculum must reflect 2SLGBTQ+ lives and realities.[17]

Even in schools and on school boards and within districts – even whole provinces – where such cultural and educational change has been undertaken, these changes have been met with initial resistance as well as support. Some members of the community resist measures that make schools safer and more inclusive for 2SLGBTQ+ students on the grounds that such programs and policies infringe on religious freedoms, arguing against these kinds of initiatives when proposed. But research has established that nothing less than a major transformation of school climate will suffice in order to create safe and inclusive schools.[18]

The initiatives to permit GSAs in Ontario and Manitoba did not occur in a vacuum. In 2011, the year preceding Ontario's introduction of *Bill 13*, the results of the *First National Climate Survey on Homophobia, Biphobia, and Transphobia in Canadian Schools* was published.[19] This first-ever national study reported on widespread harassment of 2SLGBTQ+ students in schools and suggested measures that could be taken to combat this form of harassment. Almost four thousand students from across Canada participated in the survey, reporting on their experiences at school and also of any institutional responses they might have experienced. The report also included recommendations for inclusive school policies. The issue of the experience of

2SLGBTQ+ students in schools and their rights was firmly on the radar, leading to a domino effect of provincial responses.

Strategies to promote the security and to protect the rights of vulnerable populations requires a sensitivity to their realities "on the ground," and an ability to gain trust and establish communication with members of those vulnerable populations. This can be done only by using law and policy not to combat individual, isolated incidents of bullying and harassment but as instruments of cultural change.

Official laws, policies, and codes of behaviour are a necessary first step. Nonetheless, what schools must do to ensure the safety of 2SLGBTQ+ students is to educate and re-educate the various actors in the setting.

Students who are 2SLGBTQ+, often by their very presence, challenge dominant gender and/or sexuality boundaries – not only for other students but also for teachers and administrators. New policies aimed at 2SLGBTQ+-inclusive education will succeed only when administrators – buttressed by the teachers who support these students and their efforts – rethink what it means to make schools safe.

In the end, however, the most important contribution to new policies will be the voices of the students themselves.

3
Voices That Matter

Prom night is a cultural and developmental milestone.

For students, high school prom is a time of self-expression, reflecting their movement from youth to adulthood. For most students on the dance floor, statements are made through their hairstyles, dresses, formal attire, corsages, and often by choice of date.

Marc Hall, a seventeen-year-old gay student at Monsignor John Pereyma Catholic Secondary School in Ontario, was like a lot of other students. He planned to attend his prom and he intended to express himself.

Marc Hall wanted to go to his prom with his boyfriend.

But his principal, Mr. Powers, said no. The principal's reason for refusing Marc Hall's request was simple, if misguided. Powers regarded the interaction of prom dates as a form of sexual activity. In his view, permitting same-sex dates would amount to condoning, if not endorsing, "homosexual acts" contrary to Catholic Church doctrine.

Hall appealed to the school board, but they upheld the principal's decision. So, Hall filed a lawsuit against his school, Mr. Powers, and the school board who supported his principal's decision. The legal proceedings alleged discrimination on the basis of sexual orientation contrary to the *Charter*.

What did Marc Hall want? He wanted an injunction. An injunction is a court order that would, in this case, demand that the principal permit Marc Hall to attend the dance with his boyfriend.

Hall argued that the denial of his request violated Ontario's *Education Act*, the legislation governing the management of schools and which required school boards in the province not to discriminate.

The school board, in turn, argued that any interference with the principal's decision by the court would amount to denying the school board its religious freedom.

And so, the issue at the heart of the case came down to a single question: Would allowing Marc Hall, a gay student, to attend this Catholic high school prom with his boyfriend prejudicially affect the rights of Catholic school boards to manage their schools?

INEVITABLE CLASH

Education issues by their very nature involve children and youth. When it comes to these legal claims, who speaks for them?

This issue of children's voices arises beyond educational contexts. In custody disputes, for example, the number of claimant voices is generally limited to that of the child and the parents; however, the state can legitimately claim to have a voice as mediator, speaking in some ways for the child, but only to resolve any competing claims put forward by the parents.

Education presents a much more difficult situation because there are many more possible voices speaking for the best interests of the children involved.

The situation is complicated because, in a modern context, the teacher is no longer regarded as standing in for the parent – they are, in essence, an agent of the state. Therefore, the state now has a direct role and interest in the education system in a way that was not true in the past and is not the case in a custody dispute.

The state cannot simply occupy the role of mediator. The state speaks with a complicated voice because of the number of government agencies and employees/representatives who are involved. Some of those agencies or individuals, though representing or acting for the state, may have perspectives and beliefs in these matters that are at variance with the state's position.

Furthermore, in the context of education, the interests of a child arise at both a personal and collective level. No education issue will be resolved with reference only to a particular child – the interests of all children and interested adults must also be considered. Similarly, the interests of particular parents – and of parents as a collective –

will be involved, as will the claims and interests of various groups and organizations.

This aspect of the issue is a little more complicated when a particular organization (typically a religion) is itself entrusted with providing an education to children. The entire issue becomes even more complex when the dialogue relates to the contentious areas of religion and sexuality.

Issues of religion and sexuality arise in areas of daily life. Parents, children's groups, educators and administrators are likely to hold widely differing and seemingly irreconcilable views. It is inevitable, then, that there will be challenges to hearing and responding to the multiple voices involved – especially when people with different interests argue for competing outcomes.

No single method of resolving that competition is likely to please everyone. That said, it is important that decision makers – whether the decision is made by a teacher, a school board, a government, or a court or other tribunal – be aware of and listen to these various voices. This means that different voices must be given appropriate weight.

The voices seeking to be heard can be grouped into the following categories: children, parents, the state and state actors, and groups and organizations including religions and special interest groups.

CHILDREN AND YOUTH IN LEGAL DISPUTES

As the education system most immediately affects children and youth, their direct voices are particularly important. And yet, it seems that their voices in particular encounter the most difficulties with respect to breaking through and being heard in legal disputes. There are both practical and constructed reasons as to why this is the case.

First, children lack both full and independent legal status. Others – usually a parent or parents – are assumed to be the primary voice for their children. Unlike with other legal disputes where one person speaks for another, parents are not expected or required to separate their own interests and voices from those of their children. Nor are parents asked to make any attempt to separate their own interests from the interests of their children in educational matters. Problems also arise when society's interest – or the interests of a segment of society –

disapproves or questions the decisions some parents make on behalf of their children.

There exist additional, practical reasons that account for why children face such difficulties being heard. These vary and include the great range of ages and maturity involved in the legal category of "child."

A single approach for all children and students will not and is not believed to work. In reality, many children employ a different "language" when engaging in certain discourses, particularly on fraught issues like sexuality or religion, and the law expects – and even demands – that a specific official or understandable kind of language be used in order for a voice to be given any weight in a legal proceeding. To the extent that children and youth employ such language, they may not have particularly fixed views on the matters at hand. That lack of official, formal, or acceptable language can lead to their views being dismissed.

Another obstacle is that the structures in which such discourse is conducted – hearings, public meetings, board deliberations – are *adult* structures that do not lend themselves to making children comfortable, let alone heard.

Finally, in any particular issue, the number of children implicated will probably be greater than the number of state actors or groups who want to be heard. The disparity in those numbers dilutes any individual or collective voice from youth and children.

It is clear that voices of 2SLGBTQ+ students need to be heard. They are far more often talked about, to, or over than listened to. Students have a significant interest in their own education, and it seems obvious that 2SLGBTQ+ students have great personal stakes in what transpires at their schools.

There are, of course, some well-known instances where 2SLGBTQ+ youth have made their voices heard in an educational context. The case of Marc Hall is typical in that for most cases in which a student has been or is demanding to be heard, they are often in their last year of high school and are nearing adulthood.[1] In his equally well-publicized case, Azmi Jubran brought forth his legal action after having endured harassment and abuse for five years.[2]

In cases such as these, the students who speak out often have supportive parents. In others, however, particularly those involving issues of sexuality in schools where children are impacted, there is a notable absence of youthful voices.[3]

NOT LISTENING

Student voices were not heard when Surrey, BC, teacher James Chamberlain sought to introduce into his school district three books dealing with same-sex parents.[4] The Surrey School Board refused to permit the introduction of the books and the case received national attention before the Supreme Court of Canada.

Student voices were not heard in 2001 when the British Columbia College of Teachers (BCCT) refused to confer teaching credentials on candidates from Christian-based Trinity Western University (TWU), a private BC institution associated with the Evangelical Free Church of Canada.[5] The British Columbia College of Teachers refused to approve the application because it was contrary to the public interest for them to approve a teacher education program that followed discriminatory practices.

Trinity Western University sought to qualify teachers who had, when first admitted to the university, signed the university's admissions covenant agreeing to abstain from all sex outside of heterosexual marriage. But not a single voice of any student was heard throughout their arguments.

Not surprisingly, Trinity Western objected, and a legal battle ensued. The case received national attention, but no students were heard from in the courtrooms making the decision.

This third example drives home the point we're trying to make. Christopher Kempling was a teacher in British Columbia. He was suspended by the British Columbia College of Teachers and disciplined by the Quesnel School District for homophobic and discriminatory comments about 2SLGBTQ+ people that he made in letters to the editor of the *Quesnel Cariboo Observer*.[6]

The dispute brought Kempling's right to freedom of expression into conflict with the equality rights of 2SLGBTQ+ students and staff. At the end of the day, in balancing the two competing rights, the court ruled that any limitations on Kempling's right to expression were justified by the school district's obligation to maintain a discrimination-free environment.

Again, no students were heard from.

The voices of students are consistently silent or absent in all of these cases, even though it is students who are at the heart, and who most keenly feel the impact, of the conduct under review.

PROTECTING THE SYSTEM NOT THE CHILD

All sides in these cases sought out and heeded the words of experts and other witnesses who spoke to the *impact* these situations had or would have on students, but without actually hearing from any students themselves. This displacement of the voices of children and youth was underscored by references to harms done to a "system's integrity," rather than to the integrity of the students.

As children often have little or no actual or direct voice in situations that explicitly affect them, the practice of adults speaking "on their behalf" is thought to be natural or even inevitable.[7] But parents speaking for young people is problematic when such situations involve sexuality and identity, especially when it comes to 2SLGBTQ+ youth.

Even when adults – such as child-welfare advocates – prove capable of detaching their own interests from those of the child or children they endeavour to support, they often do not possess the immediate complexity of being of a 2SLGBTQ+ child and/or are not aware that the possibility of such a distinction could exist. In these situations, the hearing of children's voices must occur. When a 2SLGBTQ+ child or youth is afforded the opportunity to speak, it is important that the process involved be crafted so as to allow them to do so in their own words and to be listened to genuinely.

To accomplish this, the legal process may require a change in structure or in the usual rules governing evidence. It is not novel that some of the law's processes may have to change in order to protect and include vulnerable people.

Anonymity may be required. The use of media – such as social media – as a process with which children are more familiar and comfortable might have to come into play as well. The use of common legal approaches to questions, cross-examination, or confinement to specific issues at hand may have to be curtailed or even eliminated.

Such special processes might well slow down or complicate any decision-making efforts, but that is a far better outcome than having a process unfold in which the children are not actually directly heard. Because an inclusive process is not just one in which children can speak and be heard but also one that meaningfully informs them of the substance of the issue or issues being discussed and the process that has been created for them.

It must be acknowledged that children have rights separate from their parents. This is particularly true in cases in which parents could have interests contrary to those of their children. Those divergent interests are not uncommon in relation to a number of issues that impact the lived realities of 2SLGBTQ+ children and youth. This can certainly be true around the issue of participating in GSAs. In these instances, a limitation on the involvement of parents should be considered.

THE ALBERTA TWO-STEP: *BILL 24* AND *BILL 8*

We have seen in Manitoba and Ontario the forward-thinking efforts to manifest in law the right of students to establish a GSA in their respective schools, along with the right to use said moniker for the club.

The journey to requiring GSAs in schools in Alberta has been more circuitous and fraught by parental opposition and resistance by school authorities. As the provincial government has switched from Conservative to NDP and then back to Conservative, attitudes toward GSAs in schools have, to put it mildly, diverged.

In 2015, in response to public pressure, the Alberta Progressive Conservative government enacted *Bill 10*,[8] amending that province's *School Act*.[9] The purpose of the amendment was to permit students to establish GSAs. The stated reason was to promote welcoming, respectful, and safe school climates – just the sort of proactive stance 2SLGBTQ+ students and their allies had been calling for. However, there were a lot of questions about just how the GSAs would operate and whether or not a school could require a GSA to meet away from it.

In 2017, the Alberta provincial government switched hands, and Premier Rachel Notley's NDP government introduced *Bill 24*,[10] which crafted very strong protections for 2SLGBTQ+ students participating in GSAs. One of the most controversial provisions prohibited principals from disclosing to parents (or to the peers of students) the fact that a student chose to participate in a GSA. That provision started a debate in Alberta that would be ongoing, pitting legal protections for students participating in GSAs against a parent's right to know and decide on their child's behalf. As a result, some parents, private religious schools, and school boards wanted a hearing on whether or not *Bill 24* was "constitutional" or legal. Their arguments were grounded in religion-based claims.

In April 2018, until that full hearing could be held, the individuals and groups opposing *Bill 24* sought an "interim" court order prohibiting implementation of *Bill 24*. They argued that *Bill 24* violated their right to freedom of religion and asked for certain provisions to be delayed until the constitutionality of the bill could be determined.

The arguments of the parents complaining about *Bill 24* were not new.

Relying on section 7 of the *Charter* and the *Alberta Bill of Rights*, the parents argued that *Bill 24* undermined the safety of their children, deprived parents of choice in the education of their children, and interfered with the right of parents to be fully informed of the activities in which their children participate.

Parents, schools, and school boards argued that *Bill 24* interfered with their collective ability to educate their children in accordance with their moral and religious values and, therefore, infringed on their parental and institutional rights to freedom of religion, expression, and association – as protected by section 2 of the *Charter*. They wanted implementation of *Bill 24* delayed.

Their request for a delaying order – the injunction – was denied.[11]

A full hearing on the constitutionality of *Bill 24* never happened.

However, what the Alberta trial court and Court of Appeal said about *Bill 24* in relation to the requested injunction or delay was very helpful in understanding the new position of 2SLGBTQ+ kids in school. In their rulings, the Alberta courts underscored the importance that Canada's courts now placed on 2SLGBTQ+ safety and inclusion, and exemplify how far 2SLGBTQ+ rights have moved prodigiously forward.

At the trial level, the application was heard by Justice Johnna C. Kubik. She reviewed evidence tendered by both sides, including evidence from pediatric experts, parents, educators, teachers, school board members, school administrators, doctors, and Ministry of Education staff.

Justice Kubik was asked to deal with the thorny issue of the alleged "right" of a parent to be informed if their child decided to participate in a GSA.[12] The parents involved in the legal action sought to prevent, in particular, the operation of a legislative provision that would have precluded schools' informing parents of their children's involvement in GSAs.

In this instance, the court acknowledged that the rights of parents were now engaged:

> In this case, it is clear, that the Charter rights of parents come into direct conflict with the Charter rights of children and, in particular, those rights to free expression, association, life, liberty, security, and equality."[13]

However, in weighing the negative impact on parental rights on one hand, and the benefits to 2SLGBTQ+ students on the other, Justice Kubik, as most courts will do, clearly and easily decided in favour of the students. Why?

The conflict between the two rights claims came down to this question: Do the benefits of the educational initiative in support of GSAs outweigh any negative effects on freedom of religion, expression, or other liberty rights of the parents?

When some parents and schools oppose GSAs, the competition between conflicting religion-based rights claims comes down to a specific inquiry: Do the benefits of addressing the marginalization of 2SLGBTQ+ students – for example, mandating GSAs in schools – outweigh any negative effects on an individual or community's expression of their religious beliefs or practices?

The court acknowledged that the liberty rights of parents were engaged on the issue of parental notification. The court also conceded that parents have the right to make fundamental decisions for their children. However, notwithstanding these fundamental parental rights,

Justice Kubik nonetheless noted that when a school makes a decision with respect to the rights of parents, "those decisions must also be in the children's best interests."[14]

Tellingly, at least in the context of a test for the granting of an interim injunction and in the context of these facts in Alberta, the court ruled that "the public good in maintaining the legislation"[15] *outweighed* allegations of harm to parents' liberty rights.

The public good referred to by the court included the documented effects on those students attending GSAs such as improved school performance, increased sense of safety and belonging, enhanced psychological well-being, and reduced drug use.[16]

Justice Kubik concluded:

> The balance of convenience weighs in favour of maintaining the legislation. The effect on 2SLGBTQ+ students in granting an injunction, which would result in both the loss of supportive GSAs in their schools and send the message that their diverse identities are less worthy of protection, would be considerably more harmful than temporarily limiting a parent's right to know and make decisions about their child's involvement in the GSA.[17]

Justice Kubik's decision was appealed in the Alberta Court of Appeal. At the Court of Appeal, the court considered evidence that was not available at the time Justice Kubik considered the case. Specifically, several months after Justice Kubik's decision, the province indicated an intention to defund or de-accredit schools[18] that failed to comply with the requirements introduced to Alberta's *School Act* by *Bill 24*.

The Court of Appeal considered this new evidence and the harm this would cause to schools seeking exemption from the GSA requirements. The court said:

> The evidence of the good achieved by GSAs in protecting the safety and privacy interests of individual children is more compelling than the new evidence of schools' termination of funding for non-compliance with the legislation. In this instance, the balance of convenience tips in favour of upholding the legislation

pending a full hearing on the merits of its constitutionality, not granting an interim injunction.[19]

In preferring the legal situation of 2SLGBTQ+ students over their parents, and the arguments of the schools and school boards, Justice Kubik took an evidence-based approach to balancing the rights of both sides. Justice Kubik pointed to expert evidence that demonstrated – and condemned – the climate in schools that 2SLGBTQ+ students faced every day. She found in support of climate-changing measures that programs such as GSAs did more than just respond to this hostile school climate. The evidence demonstrated that:

- 70 percent of all students, 2SLGBTQ+ and non-2SLGBTQ+, reported hearing epithets every day, such as "that's so gay," and nearly half (48 percent) heard pejorative comments daily, such as "faggot," "lezbo," and "dyke."
- Nearly 10 percent of 2SLGBTQ+ students reported hearing homonegative comments from teachers daily or weekly.
- 74 percent of transgender students, 55 percent of other 2SLGBTQ+ students, and 26 percent of non-2SLGBTQ+ students experienced verbal harassment regarding their gender expression.
- 68 percent of transgender students, 55 percent of female sexual-minority students, and 42 percent of male sexual-minority students reported experiencing verbal harassment regarding their perceived gender or sexual orientation.
- 21 percent of 2SLGBTQ+ students reported being physically harassed or assaulted due to their sexual orientation.
- 64 percent of 2SLGBTQ+ students and 61 percent of students with 2SLGBTQ+ parents reported that they felt unsafe in Canadian schools.[20]

As to the outcomes of negative school climate if unchecked, the court reiterated the findings of the experts:

> [S]tudies have shown that homophobia results in 2SLGBTQ+ students having higher rates of suicidal ideation than heterosexual students, lower grades, lower progress to post-secondary

education, higher rates of skipping school because of safety concerns, higher rates of risky behaviour, and higher rates of depression and suicidal ideation than non-2SLGBTQ+ students. The direct anecdotal evidence of teachers and 2SLGBTQ+ youth who participated in GSAs bears out these statistics.[21]

AND ONE STEP BACK

There was no full hearing of the merits of the case – that is, a final determination of whether or not *Bill 24* would have been upheld on its constitutional merits. Our view is that it would likely have been upheld. The failure of the parents and the schools to secure their order to be granted immediate exemption from the requirements of *Bill 24* should not be confused with the last word on the matter.

In the 2019 provincial election, Alberta's United Conservative Party (UCP) won a majority of seats, sweeping the NDP out of office. In turn, following through on promises made on the campaign trail, the UCP swept *Bill 24* aside, replacing it with *Bill 8*.[22]

What did *Bill 8* do? *Bill 8* rolled back some of the legal protections contained in *Bill 24*, particularly the provision that had prohibited school staff from disclosing student involvement in GSAs. The fear, of course, is that students will refrain from joining a GSA if there is even a remote possibility that their parents will be informed.[23]

Under the new bill, there was no requirement for principals to permit students to "immediately" form a GSA should they request one. Schools would now determine timelines; although the government claimed they would be on alert for any schools where a principal might be unreasonably delaying things. Also gone was the right to use the words "gay" or "queer" in the name of the GSA or group – rights already guaranteed in Manitoba and Ontario.[24]

While the general course of the law has been moving resolutely forward, *Bill 8* is a signal that there will still be setbacks. We are of the view that these setbacks are temporary.

Protection against disclosure of a student's membership in a GSA would now rely entirely on Alberta's privacy laws.[25] The privacy protections in *Bill 24* were superior – rolling them back was the greatest failing of *Bill 8*. The potential harms in permitting schools to inform parents of their child's participation in a GSA are real and unpredictable.

However, Alberta's privacy laws are not entirely toothless.

For example, in order for a school to disclose a student's engagement with a GSA, there must be a reason. Parents can be notified only to "avert or minimize a risk of harm to the health or safety of a minor."[26] Whether or not this opens the door to schools informing parents of their child's involvement with a GSA simply because they think it best to do so remains to be seen and is concerning.

In theory, a school may disclose personal information about a student "only to the extent necessary to enable it to carry out its purpose in a reasonable manner."[27] Therefore, there are qualifications and limitations to what may be divulged, but again the language raises a question about its application.

Passage of *Bill 8* is a reminder that rights and legal gains must be protected by the vigilant. When *Bill 8* was enacted, dozens of members of the 2SLGBTQ+ community and their allies protested both at the legislature and on the steps of Calgary City Hall.[28] Janis Irwin, NDP Member of Provincial Parliament, made clear that the NDP opposition was "not giving up the fight."[29] She said: "There are a lot of kids who aren't safe in their schools and in their classrooms – teachers and staff as well – so we need to change that ... I think this [protest] sends a really strong message to this UCP government that as much as they would like this issue to disappear ... it's not going to."[30]

LIMITATIONS OF THE LAW

There are now three provinces in Canada – Ontario, Manitoba, and Alberta – with legislation in place granting students, with varying degrees of protections, the right to establish a GSA in their school[31]; however, there is still, as a necessary part of these approaches, a burden of responsibility unfairly placed on the backs of students – most of whom will be 2SLGBTQ+ – to come forward and self-identify as a "sexual outlaw," which can be intimidating and silencing.

Heterosexual students who wish to establish a GSA also take a risk in that they, too, may be thought of as 2SLGBTQ+ or simply ridiculed for their support. In either case, they, too, may find themselves subject to harassment.

The right in the legislation is imbued in the students and not the teachers – an unfortunate consequence of legislation that is otherwise intended to change the culture of schools. A better approach to be considered by other jurisdictions as they might consider legislation of their own is one that involves indirect initiation. This would mean having school officials facilitate the progress of GSAs, but via a process that includes student voices. Such an approach would require schools and school officials to be particularly attentive to possible student interests or requirements. That in itself might prove a challenging task when confronted by school officials who may not be conscious of the needs of students in matters related to minority sexualities and gender identity.

Initiating a legal process by a student without the involvement and/or approval of a parent will be especially difficult.

It should not be left to students to create the discourse with respect to such groups or spaces. To do so may require students to identify themselves more than they are ready or able to do. To require a student who initiates legal action to have a particular sexual or gender self-identification is far too onerous a requirement and will ensure that the student's voice is not heard.

In any event, many students have not actually committed to any particular sexual or gender self-identification, which is one of the values of the GSAs – and, in fact, of more general recent attitudes to sexuality – particularly among youth.

It can be difficult enough for any student to be involved in a GSA, let alone to be responsible for initiating the required action in establishing a GSA. This point has been recognized in some legal decisions. In the human rights context, the decision in the *Jubran* case constitutes a rejection that protection on the basis of sexual orientation can be accorded only to somebody who identifies with the sexual orientation being discriminated against.[32]

In ruling that it was not necessary for Azmi Jubran to be "homosexual" to seek legal protection from homophobic harassment, the court emphasized how difficult it can be for young people to make a complaint when the issue in dispute relates to their sexuality.

The court was quite specific: "The chambers judge's interpretation of s. 8 would impose an unwarranted burden on a person such as Mr. Jubran to either declare himself as a homosexual or prove that his harassers believed him to be homosexual."[33]

If parents are required to be involved or consulted (as legal representatives) when their child initiates legal action, then the voices of many students will not be heard. Some parents will be hostile to the very presence of a GSA in their child's school – to say nothing of permitting their child to lead a discourse initiative to set up a GSA.

This issue can partly be addressed by having other adults, not necessarily parents, involved in the creation of a GSA. Such adults or their groups or organizations cannot, however, fully substitute for the authentic voice of the children involved. Children and youth must be among those who speak on their behalf and not just objects of discussion. Like Gabe Picard and Azmi Jubran, they must be heard – and seen to be heard.

LISTENING TO PARENTS

Parental control over children's upbringing and education in Canada has deep roots. In *Chamberlain*,[34] the case dealing with the banning of books depicting same-sex parenting, the Supreme Court observed that "[t]he common law has long recognized that parents are in the best position to take care of their children and make all the decisions necessary to ensure their well-being."[35]

The parental right to educate children is also protected by two provisions of the *Charter*. First, a parent's right to freedom of religion and conscience is guaranteed under s 2(a), encompassing the right to educate one's child according to those beliefs. In addition, the parental right to control a child's religious and moral education is protected by section 7 of the *Charter*.[36]

The Supreme Court described this protection in *Chamberlain* in the following terms:

> our society is far from having repudiated the privileged role parents exercise in the upbringing of their children. This role translates into a protected sphere of parental decision-making

which is rooted in the presumption that parents should make important decisions affecting their children both because parents are more likely to appreciate the best interests of their children and because the state is ill-equipped to make such decisions itself. Moreover, individuals have a deep personal interest as parents in fostering the growth of their own children.[37]

However, the parental right to educate, whether supported by the common law or the *Charter*, is not an absolute right. Furthermore, that protection is premised on the notion that "[p]arents will be presumed to be acting in their children's 'best interests' – unless the contrary is shown."[38] The state will intervene only when parental conduct falls below a "socially acceptable threshold."[39]

It is true that the voices and interests of parents have been separated from those of their children in some contexts. Parental religious objections to matters such as medical treatment, for example, have been overridden in the past on the basis of the "best interests" of the child.[40]

It is unlikely, however, that such legal authorities will have much application in the context of education. This is true no matter how unhelpful a parent's decisions might be for the mental or emotional health or development of a particular child. In most contexts, parents will be the primary voices for their children, including in educational matters. Sometimes this has express legal manifestations, including in contexts relating to issues of sexuality and gender.

● ● ● ● ● ● ●

KEY CASE
Chamberlain v Surrey School District No 36
2002 SCC 86

The Supreme Court acknowledged that marginalization of students can result from a use of selective religious views to determine actions by or on behalf of the state – in this case, determining which books to include or exclude from school curriculum.

● ●

In many cases, and particularly when a child is very young, the voice of the parent is usually the only voice the law considers or empowers to speak on behalf of the child. On other matters, however, and especially as the child gets older, it is more problematic.

Greatly complicating the position for many 2SLGBTQ+ children is the hostile environment they face at home. This hostility can arise well before they are old enough to attend school. For example, in the case of *Halton Children's Aid Society v G.K.*, a custody dispute involving two children aged three and four,[41] the main issue was related to a dispute between the parents about the gender identity of their older child. The father argued that the mother was forcing the boy to dress as a girl, and the mother argued that the father rejected the child's desire to identify as a girl.

The difficult position of the child was illustrated through expert medical evidence. Dr. Bonafacio, a specialist in gender issues, said: "... [The child] is acutely aware of the conflict between his parents and their differing views about his gender expressions or identity. [The child] is no doubt aware of his father's views about ... variant gender expressions. [The child] loves both parents very much [and] wishes to please both parents and make them both happy."[42]

The judge accepted this evidence, adding "... each parent needs to permit [the child] a variety of ways of expressing himself and ... should be supported but not encouraged toward any gender preference."[43] The judge acknowledged that both parents could be causing the child "emotional harm."[44]

Parents in situations involving 2SLGBTQ+ children may be averse to having a child exposed to or involved in supportive situations at school. They may find support from parents' groups that also take such obstructionist stances.

For example, in Prince George in the late 1980s, a parents' group succeeded in getting a book called *Boys and Sex* banned from the senior secondary school library.[45] They succeeded in part because the book's discussion of homosexuality was found to be "inappropriate."[46]

The parents feared that the book would "undermine children's faith in both their parents and in religion."[47] That decision, however, was a long time ago. It preceded the recognition of sexual orientation as grounds for protection in the *Charter*, the introduction of same-sex marriage in Canada, and the very specific cases dealing with the rights of 2SLGBTQ+ students in schools.

In Alberta, parents argued that GSAs were harmful to students:

> GSAs are harmful [in] that children in GSAs are exposed to inappropriate, sexually explicit information, as well as information about gender and sexuality, which is either harmful in its own right, ideological in nature or contrary to the parents' and schools [sic] beliefs regarding such matters.[48]

Even after the Supreme Court of Canada ruled that the banning of the same-sex parenting books in the *Chamberlain*[49] case was unlawful, the court nonetheless accepted that parents and parents' groups would continue to play a large role in school decisions.

Some parents will certainly object to their child or children having a direct voice in any discourse not the same as or consonant with their own. As in the Prince George and *Chamberlain* situations, the claims and voices of parents may be made on the basis that failing to include them will undermine the religious ideas they are trying to instill within their homes.

Fortunately, Canadian courts have been averse to "sheltering" children from voices at school that are not necessarily consonant with those they hear at home. This was recognized in both the *Chamberlain* and the *SL v Commission* cases at the Supreme Court of Canada.

Chamberlain addressed the issue of whether or not to allow into the curriculum books that dealt with same-sex parents.

SL v Commission addressed whether students could be required to take a course that studied a variety of religions in society – including atheism.

Both decisions are worth quoting at length.

In giving her reasons in *Chamberlain*, Chief Justice McLachlin said:

> ... although parental involvement is important, it cannot come at the expense of respect for the values and practices of all members of the school community ... The number of different family models in the community means that some children will inevitably come from families of which certain parents disapprove.

> Giving these children an opportunity to discuss their family models may expose other children to some cognitive dissonance. But such dissonance is neither avoidable nor noxious. Children encounter it every day in the public-school system as members of a diverse student body. They see their classmates, and perhaps also their teachers, eating foods at lunch that they themselves are not permitted to eat, whether because of their parents' religious strictures or because of other moral beliefs.[50]

In *SL v Commission scolaire*,[51] Justice Deschamps expressed a similar opinion:

> Parents are free to pass their personal beliefs on to their children if they so wish. However, the early exposure of children to realities that differ from those in their immediate family environment is a fact of life in society. The suggestion that exposing children to a variety of religious facts in itself infringes their religious freedom or that of their parents amounts to a rejection of the multicultural reality of Canadian society and ignores the Quebec government's obligations with regard to public education.[52]

As Justice Kubik noted in the Alberta GSA dispute: "GSAs are voluntary student organizations. Children are not required to participate in them. The Act in no way restricts the right of parents or schools to continue to impart their religious and moral values to their children."[53]

ONE ROLE, MANY VOICES

One of the difficulties in giving undue weight to the voices of parents is that there will be many such voices and they will not all be able to be reconciled.

In reality, some of those parent voices will be very loud, persistent, and insistent, but not in any sense representative of either the majority of parents or students, or of fundamental social values such as equality and inclusiveness. Because of the insistence of such voices, however, they may be given undue weight within the discourse.

● ● ● ● ● ● ●
KEY CASE
Ross v New Brunswick School District No 15

The Supreme Court of Canada confirmed that a school is a communication centre for a whole range of values and aspirations of a society. The school is an arena for the exchange of ideas and must, therefore, be premised upon principles of tolerance and impartiality so that all persons within the school environment feel equally free to participate. A school board has a duty to maintain a positive school environment for all persons served by it.

● ●

Quite apart from the undesirability of parental influence in some matters – for example, denying children access to groups such as GSAs – is the fact that opposition would be difficult to put into operation. Some parents, for religion or for other reasons, will want the GSAs set up.

Parents will simply not agree on what action should be taken. Many, for example, will have opposing views based on different religions. The obvious intra-religion conflict this sets up alone precludes a definitive voice for any particular parent.

Chamberlain is again a helpful case here. Justice LeBel, in concurring majority reasons, remarked on the marginalization that can follow from a use of selective religious views to determine actions by or on behalf of the state. He gave an example:

> The incompatibility of the views expressed in the affidavits with the principles of secularism and non-sectarianism would perhaps be even more apparent if the parents had objected to the portrayal of families of a particular religious background – Muslim families, for example. No doubt the practices of Muslims are contrary to the teachings of some other religions; indeed, their beliefs are deeply opposed to those of some other religions. But Christian or Hindu parents could not object (unless they renounced any claim that their objections were

non-sectarian) to the mere presence of a Muslim family in a story book, or the mere intimation that happy, likeable Muslim families exist, on the basis that Muslims do and believe some things with which they do not agree, or that encountering these stories might bring children face to face with the reality that not everyone shares their parents' beliefs.[54]

Furthermore, as the courts in *Chamberlain* and *SL v Commission* stressed, there needs to be some point of commonality in an educational system. A key decision from the Supreme Court of Canada, *Ross v New Brunswick School District No. 15*, makes this important point:

> In large part, [a school] defines the values that transcend society through the educational medium. The school ... must, therefore, be premised upon principles of tolerance and impartiality so that all persons within the school environment feel equally free to participate. As the Board of Inquiry stated, a school board has a duty to maintain a positive school environment for all persons served by it and it must be ever vigilant of anything that might interfere with this duty. It is not sufficient for a school board to take a passive role.[55]

That passage was cited approvingly in *Chamberlain*. To it, the court added the following:

> In my saying that parents do and ought to have input at the local level with regard to the values which their children receive in school, I want to make it clear that this does not amount to, as alleged in submissions before this Court, that a particular parent or group of parents has a 'veto' over the local delivery of the provincial curriculum.[56]

In considering the numerous observations of the Supreme Court of Canada on the issue of the role of parents, it seems a reasonable position to insist that no process should bestow upon parents an unlimited power of veto. This extends to whether a child can participate in some discourses or in activities that result from a particular discourse such as the establishment of a GSA.

Schools have been and are run by reference to parents' views on particular matters, but not pursuant to parents' views. Parents have rights, but parents should not have an unfettered space for their uncontradicted or unqualified voices.

The law has been arching in a direction that ensures that they do not.

4
"What's New?"

DEALING WITH PRECONCEPTIONS

Legal rules and decisions from the courts are often created and based upon conceptions of religion and sexuality specific to a particular time and place. What was believed to be "the case" in the 1990s, for example, does not hold true twenty years later.

However, the cultural reasons for our preconceptions about various religions can be quite different from the myriad sources responsible for our rigid thinking about gender and sexuality.

It is not surprising that there are fixed conceptions – legal or otherwise – about religion.

Religions have long been a focal point of social, political, and legal contention. In particular, religion is often associated with inflexible views on various social and legal issues. These positions have, in some cases, been developed over considerable time despite an assumption that these views are unchanging outside of a period of profound general social upheaval.

Sexuality and gender have been subject to various imposed norms and taboos over time. These imposed norms have sought to deny certain sexualities, or forms of sexual expression, and identities from existing at all ("we have no gays") or from being expressed (the suppression of 2SLGBTQ+ groups, newspapers, websites, and protests and the imposition of rigid gender codes).

The one constant has been a tendency to try to standardize gender and sexual expression and to suppress all "other" (i.e., inferior) forms.

In western culture, except for traditional perspectives that conceptualize heterosexuality as dominant, there is no "ancient" or "time immemorial" concept of other, different sexualities. Social norms, values, belief systems, customs and, especially, religions have taken a leading role in establishing models and precedents for gender and sexuality expression while suppressing even the acknowledgment of, or conversations about, other possibilities or long-present identities and realities. This process of suppression continues today. Obvious current examples include religion-driven hysteria about homosexuality in Nigeria and Uganda, as well as church-backed laws in Russia that purport to prohibit homosexual "propaganda" aimed at youth.

How do we make space for more robust understandings of religions, sexualities and gender identities?

In matters of religion, gender and sexuality, law recognizes and protects, what is for law, "new" voices. These voices have been raised most recently in the ongoing dialogues around safety, inclusion and equality rights in schools. The conversations in Canada on the issues of gender, sexuality and religion in schools have been infused with traditional Christian religious thought and the binary of homosexuality and heterosexuality. Existing law and literature, then, has had little to say about *all* religions, *all* sexualities, and *all* gender identities. The variety of membership in each of these areas cannot be underestimated.

The sexuality and gender context includes 2SLGBTQ+ and questioning persons, trans individuals (including those who are binary transgender, transsexual, non-binary, agender, androgynous, gender-fluid, intersex, and two-spirit), and those who are bisexual, asexual, and/or polyamorous. Those who embody these identities will need novel types of spaces in any discourse and cannot simply be assimilated into heterosexuality or homosexuality.

A great part of the challenge in welcoming and celebrating the new involves basic recognition of the preconceptions that already exist. There is a tendency to use such preconceptions as part of a process to make legal issues comprehensible and to address them efficiently; however, such processes can make it difficult for those seeking legal recognition or protection to find space and to position themselves so that they can be heard on their own terms – and not be treated as just "imitations" of established or "accepted" groups.

Once preconceptions are acknowledged they can be avoided as legal standards. The avoidance of these preconceptions can then serve as a jumping off point to creating a meaningful space for those who are new to law's horizon or those who come seeking something new.

This approach is consistent with the educational aims of inquiry and questioning and also with the lack of fixed identity that characterizes youth culture. Schools should be places for encouraging fluidity of definition and challenging preconceptions.

Such an expectation does not gut the idea of a uniform set of social and legal values being instilled in schools and elsewhere. Instead, it is the very fulfilment of the equality guarantees in the *Charter* and a true example of a diverse culture in action.

In this way, those who approach law seeking equality and inclusion are not just accommodated but also celebrated.

RELIGION-BASED CLAIMS

Suppression and the regularization of sexuality is manifested in such issues as same-sex marriage[1] and opposition to GSAs.[2] Religion-based legal claims are often about finding space for a particular religion in a particular place.[3] This preconception about religion – that religion is entitled to a place – is often unchallenged because it has become so much the norm.

In the context of schools, the uncontested nature of a religion claim is particularly striking. For example, religion-based claims can be asserted, requiring other people – people who do not subscribe to the religion in question – to bear the consequences of the creation of a space for said religion.[4] These kinds of claims impact how other, non-religious persons, especially children and youth, access knowledge and services or navigate certain interactions.

Religion claims may well amount to claims that require others to comport themselves in accordance with a specific religious tradition. Examples would be not to marry a person of the same sex, not to bring a date of the same sex to one's prom,[5] not to identify as lesbian if you want to work with a specific person,[6] not to have access to books depicting same-sex parents,[7] and not to have groups such as GSAs.[8]

FORMAL EQUALITY

The belief that all people must be treated exactly alike in order to achieve fairness. In this view, it is variation in treatment that creates inequality and unfairness.

SEXUALITY CLAIMS

There is a fundamental difference between claims dealing with sexuality on the one hand, and claims grounded in freedom of religion on the other. Claims based on sexuality are not projected onto others in terms of effect. Instead, they are claims to provide accommodation to those asserting the claim, but not limiting the space accorded to others as religion-based claims often do.

Examples would be: my marriage does not preclude yours, my books do not exclude yours, my prom date does not keep you from bringing yours.

This is a significant difference.

Furthermore, sexual orientation claims do not try to close the door to the sexual orientation claims of others. Claims to have inclusive school materials on same-sex marriages or same-sex parents do not exclude the existence of materials on heterosexuality or transgender identity.

SUBSTANTIVE EQUALITY

The belief that treating everyone "the same" will not, in fact, result in fairness or equality at all. Fairness and "substantive" equality can be achieved only when sexual orientation, race, gender, or other characteristics are taken into account when making efforts to achieve equality.

Why do some seek recourse in preconceptions?

On a broad level, it might be argued that fixed conceptions provide a uniform approach to rights. Complexity or fluidity in definition or content, some argue, allows only for "special" rights.

Some also complain that complex or fluid conceptions oppose the customs and traditions of the majority. These arguments are alarmist and, at best, based on an excessively formal conception of equality as opposed to substantive equality.

Formal equality is a belief that all people must be treated exactly alike in order to achieve fairness. In this view, it is variation in treatment that creates unfairness.

Substantive equality recognizes that treating everyone "the same" will not, in fact, result in fairness or equality at all. Fairness and "substantive" equality can be achieved only when sexual orientation, race, gender, or other characteristics are taken into account in ameliorating efforts to achieve equality.

Most important, arguments grounded in formal equality are inconsistent with recent human rights and court cases dealing with equality law, generally, and certainly the recent developments in legislation and case law that are defining – and empowering – 2SLGBTQ+ students in school.

ESSENTIALLY ESSENTIALIST

Fixed definitions of religion and sexuality are consistent with the idea that there is an essentialist truth to both. However simplistic, it is efficient to conceive of religion and sexuality as having an unchanging, core definition. Some seek clarity in order to protect a category or to regulate it.

Furthermore, the legal structure available for rights protection, whether for sexuality, religion, or otherwise, contains within it a distinct inclination toward essentialism. The listing of certain categories of equality rights protection in section 15 of the *Charter* (race, national or ethnic origin, colour, religion, sex, age, or mental or physical disability) is evidence of law's need to categorize.

The law has determined the importance, for example, of determining whether an action or statement alleged to be anti-Sikh is

> **ESSENTIALISM**
>
> A belief that attributes the reality or truth of something to an essence embodied in it. For example, masculine behaviour is attributed to the innate makeup of being a man as opposed to a culture that defines/produces/encourages certain behaviours, which can be modified or changed. Essentialism, then, dictates that men and women behave, essentially, in different ways.

discriminatory on the basis of religion, race, or national origin. There are several possibilities on the "list" of protected grounds. The importance of this "right" (or "wrong") categorization was referred to in a landmark decision in which the Supreme Court of Canada required that sexual orientation be included in Alberta's human rights legislation. That case, *Vriend v Alberta*, noted "the lack of success that lesbian women and gay men have had in attempting to obtain a remedy for discrimination on the ground of sexual orientation by complaining on other grounds such as sex or marital status."[9]

On a more practical level, an essentialist approach in law is often bolstered because rights issues will be partly construed as a question of numbers. In the Canadian legal system, rights tend to be taken seriously when the numbers of those affected are somewhere between the majority point and mere isolated instances.

There is a space between membership in a dominant group and the position of the individual at which conscious accommodation is both most justified and most practical. Where exactly this point is will depend on the area and the circumstances. However, in order to *count*, the law has traditionally required a degree of certainty about what, in fact, counts and what does not.

Categorization makes issues easier for the law (or other social or political institutions, for that matter) to deal with. More complex issues make the law – through apparatuses such as legislatures and courts – apprehensive about the ripple effects of what law is asked to do.

Such apparatuses, however, do not catch everyone who needs protection, leading to arguments grounded in what's considered "normal."

AN ESSENTIALIST LEGAL SYSTEM

Those who litigate, especially in contentious areas such as religion and sexuality, will attempt to simplify their case or at least to "normalize" the parties and issues involved as much as possible. For example, in the context of same-sex marriage cases, those challenging the existing law would locate themselves to be, aside from their sexuality, as "normal" as possible.[10]

The claimants should not be criminals, should not have been previously married, should not have children already, and should not be from too many other minorities (race, class, religion, and so on). Even their sexuality – the point of making the legal challenge – should not be too different from each other. They should both identify, for example, as lesbians and be of similar age and background. They should not be a sixty-year-old white man and a twenty-year-old African refugee who was previously married to a woman.

The same tendency applies when there is a claim for protection on the basis of religion. The religion issue should be fairly clear. The faith at stake should be a "known" one with a predictable quality about it and not the subject of scholarly research and expertise.

This was evident in the lengthy discussion of what experts on Christianity, Islam, and Mormonism had to say about polygamy in the *Polygamy Reference*.[11] The person claiming the protection should not be too recent a convert or too casual an adherent. There should be clarity in the religious views of the individual. The person should not be too questioning in terms of tenets of faith, especially those at issue in their particular case.

In other words, the law protects what it is more comfortable protecting.

SINCERITY (AND CLARITY) OF BELIEF

In *Amselem*, the case in Chapter 1 dealing with the right to build a succah on the balcony of an apartment building, the Supreme Court of

Canada said that sincerity of belief is not inconsistent with a change in belief.[12] Nonetheless, the law prefers that beliefs should, at least, be clear.

It is notable that in all the major cases about religion (and sexuality), the parties involved have very fixed conceptions of self.

When same-sex marriage was legalized throughout Canada in July 2005, there was a series of complaints from marriage commissioners around the country who objected to being required to perform same-sex civil marriages. In one of these cases, one of the commissioners was described as follows: "Mr. Nichols is a member of the Faith Baptist Church. In addition to serving on the Board of Trustees and on the Stewardship Board of his church, Mr. Nichols described his faith as taking 'first place' in his life. He prays and reads the Bible daily and lives his life with the Bible as his guidebook."[13]

When same-sex marriage was argued before the Court of Appeal in Quebec, Abdalla Idris Ali, Director of the Centre of Islamic Education in North America, said that a redefinition of marriage to include same-sex unions "would be directly contrary to, and invalidate our religious beliefs."[14] He added, "It would become harder for Muslims to participate in Canadian society if that society insisted on acceptance of unions that our religion teaches are an affront to Allah."[15]

Compare those cases with *Chiang v Vancouver Board of Education*. This was a human rights case involving the claim of a teacher-librarian who complained that her rights were violated when she was asked to display rainbow stickers and catalogue books of 2SLGBTQ+ interest in the school library.[16] Mrs. Chiang, the sponsor teacher for the School's Christian Fellowship Club, complained that she was put in an untenable position because she was known to be "religious." She asserted that if she did not put up the stickers she would be seen as "intolerant." Although she raised the religion issue, her claim was dismissed in part because she did not say what those views were, nor did she claim that her religion required her to not put up such stickers.[17]

In terms of legislation and litigation, the desire to give definition and certainty to the factors governing religion and sexuality can be understandable. For example, in terms of the particular parties or interest groups and issues involved, why would these plaintiffs want to complicate their cases with nuance or doubt?

However, there is long-term impact on the perception of the members of a particular group if the characteristics of certain individuals are seen as being representative of the whole. There is little room for doubt, flexibility, change, nuance, or accommodation in such situations. There is a certainty of identity, absence of nuance, a black-and-white quality that includes a perception of the world as being either heterosexual or homosexual.

SEPARATING RELIGION AND SEXUALITY

Another preconception is the distinction and separation of categories of religion and sexuality. This division is also open to question for there are some sexual identities that can also claim religious identities.[18]

An assumed separation between religion and sexuality may also lead to an unfair assumption that a person advocating for sexual orientation equality rights must be of no religion – or is not simultaneously presenting a position for religion or spirituality.

ISSUES WITH THESE PRECONCEPTIONS

Whether accurate or not, the reliance on fixed conceptions in matters of religion or sexuality causes difficulty in repositioning schools – or other institutions – to be open to other, newer conceptions.

Applying new conceptions about religion or sexuality, or new membership parameters within each, is hindered by current beliefs.

First, much of the standardization of both categories is unconscious. But within and outside both religion and our understanding of sexualities, the world is changing. To talk of religion with a presumption of Judeo-Christian histories is no longer accurate, nor is it sufficient. Even that terminology has changed. Scholars and writers are more likely today to speak of the Abrahamic religions, which include such religions as Druze and Islam in addition to Judaism and Christianity.

The homosexual/heterosexual binary is a quaint relic from the past (a not-too-distant past, it is true). The vocabulary of middle school 2SLGBTQ+ students includes self-descriptions as "pansexual" or "fluid sexuality."

Fluidity and a lack of fixed identity is the very essence of youth culture. This is especially true in terms of beliefs (religion), identity (sexuality), and the practice of either religion or sexuality.

Fixed categorizations of gender, religion and sexuality negatively impact students. This kind of inside-the-box thinking does a disservice in terms of how children and youth – and therefore schools – are legally impacted.

To set norms related to either religion or sexuality in a way that expects or is grounded in essentialism is inherently problematic. The challenges of preconceptions and fixed definitions are compounded for children and youth, who are mostly perceived as having an essential legal quality indistinct from their parents.

Even today, Canadian law is reluctant to detach children's rights from those of their parents – apart from issues of physical integrity and health.[19] Children and youth are not seen as having religious interests separate from those of their parents.[20] In fact, religion and children are thought to happily mix – in the eyes of the law but also with society at large.

But children have religion rights in schools. This was recognized in a very well-known 2006 case from Quebec, *Multani v Commission scolaire Marguerite-Bourgeoys*.[21]

In that case, a Sikh student wanted to carry a kirpan to school as an article of his faith. A kirpan is a religious object that resembles a dagger and is required to be made of metal. He believed that his religion required him to wear a kirpan at all times.

In 2001, the student, who kept the kirpan under his clothes, accidentally dropped the religious object in the schoolyard. As a reasonable accommodation, the school board authorized the student to wear his kirpan to school provided that he complied with certain conditions to ensure it was sealed inside his clothing. The student and his parents agreed to the accommodation.

However, the governing board of the school – supported by the board's council of commissioners – refused to approve the arrangement, insisting that the kirpan be made out of wood or plastic or some other acceptable material. The student and his parents would not agree to the modified arrangement and filed a legal action complaining that the decision of the councillors infringed upon the student's freedom of religion under s 2(1) of the *Charter*.

The Supreme Court was faced with deciding whether the commissioners' decision infringed on the student's freedom of religion. The court found in favour of the student – so long as certain restrictive conditions were observed and its use as a weapon was prevented, the wearing of the metal kirpan was deemed permissible.

That kind of association between youth and rights protection has taken longer to materialize in relation to sexuality and children. Historically, there has been hostility to the association of non-traditional sexuality and children, which has in turn had an impact in schools. For whatever rights 2SLGBTQ+ adults have, there is often a disinclination and sometimes outright hostility to the idea of accepting that children might be 2SLGBTQ+ or questioning.

This approach is sometimes presented as sheltering children from issues associated with sexuality in general. However, that perception ignores the relentless heterosexual messaging that students receive in all aspects of their lives.

Schools play a crucial role in heterosexual normativity. Heterosexuality is simply *assumed*; homosexuality or other minority sexualities are often, if mentioned at all, *studied*.

WHO DEFINES RELIGION?

Preconception about religion has two aspects – who defines religion and what that definition is. Religion is perceived in certain fixed ways, but a religion is also largely free to define itself.

The law shows deference to religions. This deference is not just with respect to particular tenets or beliefs but also whether or not an issue should even be characterized as religious in the first place.

If an individual chooses to characterize an objection to government action or conduct as a religious objection, the law has tended to accept that characterization readily, without much challenge.

In *Amselem*, the Supreme Court said this:

> [P]rovided that an individual demonstrates that he or she sincerely believes that a certain practice or belief is experientially

religious in nature in that it is either objectively required by the religion, or that he or she subjectively believes that it is required by the religion, or that he or she sincerely believes that the practice engenders a personal, subjective connection to the divine or to the subject or object of his or her spiritual faith, and as long as that practice has a nexus with religion, it should trigger the protection of s. 3 of the Quebec *Charter* or that of s. 2(a) of the Canadian *Charter*, or both, depending on the context.[22]

The ready acceptance by courts of an individual's characterization of an issue as interfering with their religious beliefs or practices is not as common in other legal contexts. In other contexts, there is much more discussion as to whether or not a dispute before the court has been properly characterized. That question of characterization is important because to ask the question is to initially consider whether the claim has merit. Or to put the matter another way, to accept that the characterization is a religious dispute is to empower plaintiffs and ignore other questions that should be considered.

For example, is the dispute religious in nature? Or is it, in fact, a cultural or political question?

Kimberly Nixon was a trans woman who volunteered at Vancouver Rape Relief & Women's Shelter. Vancouver Rape Relief was permitted to exclude Nixon because she presented as male for a good part of her life. There was a great deal of discussion and emphasis on the fact that Nixon was "medically a woman," as established by medical experts.[23]

In Azmi Jubran's legal proceedings, there was much discussion at the human rights tribunal and the BC Supreme Court – but not at the Court of Appeal – as to whether Jubran was or was not homosexual.[24]

In relation to the characterization of questions before the court, the law accepts too much as being religious in nature, permitting certain issues to escape critical scrutiny or regulation as a result.

Richard Moon wrote that "... even when the state is pursuing an otherwise legitimate public purpose ... it may be required to compromise this purpose and accommodate incompatible religious practices. There is no similar state obligation to accommodate non-religious beliefs and practices."[25]

Religious belief is, therefore, "special."[26]

Not surprisingly, cultural or political views might be somewhat artificially "dressed up" as religious in order to give them a higher degree of protection from scrutiny. The claims of infringement in many Christianity-based contexts thus may not be based on disputes that are particularly religious.

Going further still, even the claim that Christianity resolutely condemns homosexuality is rather misleading given the silence of New Testament texts on homosexuality and the silence of Jesus Christ on most homosexual acts, lesbianism, and gender identities.[27]

SEXUALITY AS A "MORAL ISSUE" — NOT!

The law has a different answer when it comes to who defines sexuality. Sexuality is often allowed to be characterized from the outside rather than from within.

The willingness of some courts to follow the practice of religions treating minority sexualities as a "moral" issue is objectionable. To speak about diverse sexual identities as a moral issue is, of course, to accept the religious conception that sexuality is a choice.

In *Chamberlain*, for example, when considering whether or not a school board could legally exclude books about same-sex parents, one of the justices said that "[t]he moral status of same-sex relationships is controversial: to say otherwise is to ignore the reality of competing beliefs which led to this case."[28]

This characterization has deep roots in the law. Lord Denning, one of the most celebrated judges in the history of the common law, said: "Although religion, law and morals can be separated, they are nevertheless still very much dependent on each other. Without religion there can be no morality: and without morality there can be no law ..."[29]

In other words, the equality claims of 2SLGBTQ+ persons arise from centuries of cultural condemnation that subjects them to scrutiny in ways that claims grounded in freedom of religion are not.

Transgender issues draw the starkest contrast, attracting considerable scrutiny for the person making a claim based on transgender identity.[30]

In the *Nixon* case, the decision itself contains a great amount of detail about her life and life history.[31] This level of detail is much higher than might be the case for an LGB person making a same-sex marriage claim or a religious person not wanting to officiate such a marriage.

In terms of definition, minority sexualities are typically defined by reference to the dominant sexuality, heterosexuality, and to a far lesser extent homosexuality. The issues confronting gays and lesbians are grounded in marginalization and denigration, and the pursuit of full citizenship, particularly in the context of schools.

When it comes to issues of gender identities, there is greater ignorance and misunderstanding.

Transgender identity cannot be about substituting "boy" for "girl" or vice versa because it is about questioning the meaning of said categories.[32] Trans people pursue self-identity in a world that has divided everyone into one of two genders on the basis of physical characteristics. For those who commit to relationships of anything more than the traditionally accepted two-person male-female coupling, they will find no recognition at all. In fact, they are apt to be seen as perverse or wicked – the general position of all 2SLGBTQ+ persons not so long ago.[33]

It is not usually presumed that a student is 2SLGBTQ+. By steering clear of that assumption, the possibility that a child might require and benefit from inclusive and celebratory responses is overlooked. One result of this is that there are, in fact, very few cases in Canada that involve the rights of 2SLGBTQ+ children.[34] Even in *Chamberlain*,[35] a case dealing with books depicting same-sex parents for use in primary school, and of crucial importance to 2SLGBTQ+ youth, the issues in dispute were argued between and among adults.

AN INCLUSIVE AND FLUID APPROACH

When legal issues arise, recognizing the effect of preconceptions on both sexuality and religion is the first step in overcoming their restrictiveness in sites such as schools. And the law may well be the best place to redress them.

It is quite possible that openness to fluidity and "the new" will not come from the parties involved in specific legal disputes. Plaintiffs and defendants, petitioners and claimants – the parties of legal disputes – are concerned with trying to focus the court's attention on a specific point.

Change is also unlikely to come from elected legislators. Legislators are often the source of some of the most egregiously fixed views about religion and sexuality. The ministers who championed legislation mandating GSAs are obvious exceptions. In Manitoba, for example, Minister of Education Nancy Allen was a tireless advocate for 2SLGBTQ+ students. However, since the introduction of legislation dealing with GSAs in Ontario in 2012, in Manitoba in 2013, and in Alberta in 2017, no other province has followed suit.

As a result, further changes may well have to come from the courts, from schools, and from the students themselves.

LAW'S EMBRACE OF THE NEW

The benefits of embracing fluidity of definition precludes exclusion and facilitates accommodation of both the new and the newcomer.

Law's embrace would also allow for a more greatly nuanced view of any issue, but particularly those issues surrounding 2SLGBTQ+ inclusion. The built-in quality of inquiry and depth that would accompany such an approach – and which an essentialist approach cannot afford – would greatly advance aspirational educational goals.

This newer attitude would also ensure that young people do not have to make committed decisions before they are ready, and it would afford schools considerable flexibility in terms of accommodation.

The essentialist approach prefers certainty, ancient authority, and received wisdom as the favoured characteristics in perceiving our world. Admitting to and using a fluid approach is more challenging and requires greater engagement and openness to change.

The importance of inclusion has been recognized in law. In *Vriend*, the Alberta decision that concluded that the failure to include sexual orientation in provincial human rights legislation infringed the right to equality of 2SLGBTQ+ people, the Supreme Court said:

> Perhaps most important is the psychological harm which may ensue ... Fear of discrimination will logically lead to concealment of true identity and this must be harmful to personal confidence and self-esteem. Compounding that effect is the implicit message

conveyed by the exclusion, that gays and lesbians, unlike other individuals, are not worthy of protection.[36]

This same point was made specifically in the context of education in the Marc Hall case. As Justice MacKinnon said:

> School is a fundamental institution in the lives of young people. It often provides the context for their social lives both in and outside of school hours ... Exclusion of a student from a significant occasion of school life, like the school Prom, constitutes a restriction in access to a fundamental social institution.[37]

With respect to religion in schools, inclusion must mean exposure to and knowledge of other religions. This is true even if this very exposure or knowledge conflicts with parental wishes and instructions.

In 2008, an Ethics and Religious Culture (ERC) program became mandatory in Quebec schools, replacing Catholic and Protestant programs of religious and moral instruction. Two parents asked the school board to exempt their children from the Ethics and Religious Culture course on the basis of it presenting serious harm to their children. They "sincerely believed" that they had an obligation to pass on the precepts of the Catholic religion to their children. The sincerity of their belief was not challenged and was readily accepted by the court.

These parents[38] argued that the Ethics and Religious Culture program infringed their religious expression rights by interfering with their rights to pass on their religious faith to their children. The only

KEY CASE
SL v Commission scolaire des Chênes
2012 SCC 7

The Supreme Court of Canada confirmed that infringement of a person's freedom of religion must be supported by objective evidence. A mere assertion that these rights have been offended is insufficient.

question at hand was whether the ability of the parents to observe their own practice had been interfered with.

The parents also maintained that exposing their children to specifics of several religions was confusing for them. The case went all the way to the Supreme Court of Canada, where the parents lost their claim. The Supreme Court stressed the importance of "religious neutrality" in state institutions such as schools.[39] By religious neutrality, the court meant "show[ing] respect for all postures toward religion, including that of having no religious beliefs whatsoever."[40]

Therefore, it was held to be appropriate for Quebec to establish compulsory courses in schools that underscored diverse religious traditions that exist in contemporary Canadian society. In fact, the opening lines of the Supreme Court's decision identify these new times:

> The societal changes that Canada has undergone since the middle of the last century have brought with them a new social philosophy that favours the recognition of minority rights. The developments in the area of education that have taken place in Quebec and that are at issue in this appeal must be situated within this larger context.

As for the criticism that such courses could undermine the religious message given by parents to their children, the court made one of its most critical statements in terms of embracing the new. These words have particular significance for parents and others who would object to 2SLGBTQ+-inclusive education or the establishment of GSAs in schools:

> Parents are free to pass their personal beliefs on to their children if they so wish. However, the early exposure of children to realities that differ from those in their immediate family environment is a fact of life in society. The suggestion that exposing children to a variety of religious facts in itself infringes their religious freedom or that of their parents amounts to a rejection of the multicultural reality of Canadian society and ignores the Quebec government's obligations with regard to public education.[41]

These words enlarge and expand upon the sentiments expressed in what Chief Justice McLachlin said in *Chamberlain*:

> Learning about tolerance is therefore learning that other people's entitlement to respect from us does not depend on whether their views accord with our own. Children cannot learn this unless they are exposed to views that differ from those they are taught at home.[42]

In the time between the two cases, *Chamberlain* in 2002 and *SL* in 2012, the court has moved from discussing the need for "tolerance" to an understanding of the "obligation" to include different "realities."

To characterize that journey another way, we have gone from tolerance to celebration in ten short years.

5
Making Spaces, Making Community

MAKING WAVES

Dr. Steve Tourloukis argued with his local school board – both in and out of court – for five years. The father of two children, ages four and six, Dr. Tourloukis described his family in the media as an "alternative family."[1]

Tourloukis, a member of the Greek Orthodox Church, sued the Hamilton-Wentworth District School Board in 2012. He did not approve of what was happening in school space, particularly in his children's classrooms.

According to Tourloukis, the public-school curriculum contained "false teachings."[2] He claimed that his religious beliefs required him to protect his children from such things, and asked the school board for several religious accommodations. These included being given advance notice as to when these "false teachings" were to occur so that he would have time to decide whether or not to withdraw his children from class.

Dr. Tourloukis stated that he did not object to the teaching of the "fact" that same-sex couples existed or were sometimes married. What he was especially concerned with were positive or affirming statements being made in the classroom in relation to those facts. He wanted to ensure that his children were taught about marriage and human sexuality from a perspective consistent with his biblical and Greek Orthodox teachings.[3]

These teachings were comprised of the beliefs that sexual relationships can occur only between one man and one woman, within marriage, and that not only were same-sex relations contrary to God's word but also there are only two genders, male and female.[4]

The School Board responded that it was not possible or practical to agree to everything Dr. Tourloukis was seeking. In particular, the school board was concerned that removing Dr. Tourloukis's children from the classroom would conflict with their obligation under Ontario law[5] to provide an inclusive and non-discriminatory educational program. Furthermore, given the integrated nature of the school board's curriculum, it was not possible to give Dr. Tourloukis the notice he was seeking.

ACCESS TO SPACE

The issue of use of school space has many aspects – the curriculum and the existence of groups such as gay-straight alliances are two of the most significant. They are mentioned here because GSAs and curriculum both raise the issue of parental approval informing how school space is used.

Other issues connected with facilitation, particularly with reference to sexuality and religious contexts, also require attention. While not as immediately conspicuous as curriculum and GSAs, these other issues of "school use" are part of the larger projects of inclusiveness and accessibility that should be aspirations of any school or school system.

After all, a key value for inclusive schools is accessibility to the facility itself. And in order to facilitate a learning environment in which assumptions are challenged and curiosities fed, diversity and choices are essential.

All students need to feel included, connected, and "at home" in their respective schools in order for them to be healthy and safe environments that foster development, mentorship, and full citizenship in society. And this environment cannot be dictated by parents who object to numerous inclusive and non-discriminatory enterprises regarding how schools elect to use their spaces.

Adults also need to have access to schools, both in terms of a permanent connection – employment, for example – and temporary access – to use the physical space of the school for events or to present information.

To prevent such access is to marginalize those who are being excluded. In some cases, exclusion *may* be justified. But exclusion or lack of facilitation based on preconceptions, past practices, or difference and dissonance is not consistent with an inclusive education system, and can and does have a harmful impact on youth and adults alike.

INSIDERS AND OUTSIDERS

Those with claims to accessing a school facility may be "insiders" or "outsiders." Their claims for access will relate both to the physical facility of the school and to the education system in general.

Insiders are most frequently the students who attend the school. They are entitled to feel like full community members of both the school and society. Students need to be able to utilize school spaces comfortably, safely, and equally. They also need to be able to be part of the educational and extracurricular activities that occur within school spaces.

Other insiders include the teachers, administrators, staff, and others who work "in" or "with" the space. These insiders must feel like equal members of the community of adults within the school space, secure both in terms of getting there and in pursuing their activities once they are in.

Outsiders include individuals and groups who want to use the school to present their ideas and perspectives. These outsiders could be groups or individuals connected to advocacy, assistance, and counselling, or entertainment and extracurricular activities. They may wish to enter the school while the "usual" insiders are also present, or they may not wish to be physically present but simply desire to access information or support from the school itself.

A school cannot be used as some sort of fair where a multitude of outsiders seek the attention of the students or teachers; however, thought must be given to the need to facilitate some form of access free from discrimination based on preconceptions or past practices. There needs to be scrutiny toward the use of specific standards that might result in differential treatment when deciding when, who, and how individuals and groups acquire access to a school.

Outsiders may also want access to the facility in a concrete way by being permitted to use the physical space when the usual community is not present. Use of physical space when insiders are present is the most straightforward facilitation issue to consider.

Nonetheless, care should be taken that there is not undue reliance on past practices and preconceptions.

STUDENT INSIDERS

The key constituency in any school is its students. The school is their work place, play space, and even a second home for a substantial part of their lives. The school is also a place that students do not choose to occupy but rather are required by law to attend. The purpose of attendance is to grow and learn in a safe and welcoming space. Each student needs to feel personally wanted, valued, and accommodated in a welcoming way.

Each student should come to appreciate that difference is valued, and that challenges are to be welcomed and not seen as nuisances.

Regardless of whether activities are considered mandatory or optional, schools should facilitate accessibility and inclusion. The physical space being used needs to be safe and accessible for all.

Restricting facilitation is, in fact, the exclusion of students.

CURRICULUM AND SPACE

Although perhaps not immediately apparent, implementing curriculum is a "space" issue. While traditional literary works that unquestionably reflect majority values and perspectives are valuable and ought to be retained, they should not exclusively occupy the curriculum.

Space for others, those who are new or perceived as new, is necessary.

Ministries, schools, and school boards are asked to ensure that the content of the curriculum does not omit "inside" groups or make the members of any group feel devalued or excluded.

Obviously, references in history classes should include more than just acknowledgement of dominant groups. The experience of religious minorities is also important. For example, in a study about the early forced conversions of Indigenous people to Christianity, it should not be assumed that students are familiar with Christianity. In turn, Christianity cannot be presented as a "bad thing" in and of itself as that would be just as exclusionary toward students of a Christian faith or background. Likewise, it shouldn't be assumed that the belief systems that were in place before the imposition of Christianity had no content.

To the extent that content or knowledge about Christianity is presented, so too should content or knowledge about the beliefs of Indigenous peoples – preferably from their own point of view.

With respect to literature studies, one of the challenges in presenting what's considered canon or "great" literature is that it is relentlessly heteronormative and Christian-centric in its content. In one sense, much of classic canon-centric literature (and film) is about the construction and celebration of heterosexual couples. A woman very rarely marries another woman or falls in love with her in these works – characters know and accept their gender, and act and dress accordingly. There is never any doubt or change.

The voices of religious and sexual minorities need to be heard, and not as an option or elective but as part of the required curriculum. These voices need to be heard in the same spaces where dominant voices are heard if they're to be normalized. Too often minority experiences are "dealt with" either as a "problem" to be solved or as a "unit" within a larger course in a special class or school assembly requiring little to no attendance or attention. In short, this kind of treatment is another form of marginalization.

Literature, popular culture, and history are frequent sites where heteronormativity overwhelms the subject matter at hand. But these are not the only areas that need to create space for minority voices. Whether it is math, literature, physical education, or any other subject, examples and hypothetical situations given to students should reflect our world's diversity of religions and sexualities.

We do not support a 2SLGBTQ+-inclusive curriculum that is hived off into a "special" subject detached from the rest of the usual curriculum. The general school life must include and celebrate 2SLGBTQ+ students, families and friendships, including friendships between 2SLGBTQ+ students and others.

Curriculum content must not be merely a presentation of "information" about 2SLGBTQ+ students received by heterosexual and non-2SLGBTQ+ students in their normative positions. Curriculum delivery – and the general school climate – must be inclusive, but not merely inclusive. Curriculum change must also implicate the privilege and social rank of heterosexual students. Inclusivity alone leaves privilege unchallenged. Therefore, curriculum must examine the social construction of the sexuality and gender of all students in order to contest cultural hierarchies rather than sustaining a normative order of gender and sexuality and other privileges.

SCHOOL ACTIVITIES

Outside of a given curriculum, there are school activities that students are expected to attend. These activities should not function as cultural practices that validate majority voices at the expense of minority ones. In a public school, prayers should not be recited at all, not even in a "neutral" way. For there is no neutrality available to people of no religion – another minority that must be considered.

Very often in community gatherings, prayers or moments of silence are justified by pointing out to those gathered that people may pray to or consider whatever god they choose. That ostensibly inclusive and neutral directive is, in fact, an imposition that marginalizes those students and teachers and staff of no religion.

Care should also be taken with respect to activities that require students to divide along gender lines. Whether this is for physical education classes, extracurricular activities, or simply which book students should read in English class, care is needed to facilitate all students. This is especially important if the gender of students is assumed without any self-identification expressed by the students themselves.

TRANSGENDER SPACES

The issue of navigating the physical spaces of a school is central for transgender students.

Conceptualizing access to school space along gender lines – boys' and girls' washrooms – is problematic for these students. A person's self-identification is the sole measure of that person's gender. It is not appropriate for others to question or challenge a person's gender identity or expression.

When it comes to washroom access, the issue is usually addressed on a case-by-case basis. The establishment of gender-neutral facilities is a solution for some, but for others, that response merely underscores the perceived "otherness" associated with being transgender.

Some parents complain that accommodating transgender students in this way transfers feelings of discomfort onto other students. Many people feel uncomfortable using public washrooms. This was true long before the issue of access and accommodation for transgender students became a human rights issue.

Progress on transgender issues is being made here and there, and some schools and school boards have adopted policies to accommodate transgender students. But there is still much to be done. It is important to agree that this work must not fall to transgender students alone. It is not a transgender student's responsibility to educate others.

This book argues for safe, welcoming and inclusive schools. Transgender students should be encouraged to participate in school life at their individual comfort level.

At all times, students have a right to participate in gym classes and team sports in a safe, inclusive, and respectful environment. Facilities such as change rooms and showers are addressed on a case-by-case basis. In change rooms that require students to undress in front of one another, those who desire privacy for any reason should be provided with accommodations that best meet their individual needs and privacy concerns. Upon a student's request, an alternate change location must be made available.

When participating in school activities and in class, every student, transgender or not, has the right to be addressed by their preferred name and referred to by the pronoun that corresponds to their gender identity or expression. A student should not be required, however, to commit to a pronoun, as that very requirement can, for some, be intrusive and unsettling. Equally, students and teachers and administrators must bear in mind that an official name change or gender change is not required in the case of a transgender student, nor is a change in official student records. In all areas of school life, transgender students have the right to dress appropriately and in accordance with their gender identity and/or expression and the school dress code.

Vancouver recently adopted a policy that allows a student to choose the name and pronoun that is used with reference to that student and to use gender-neutral washrooms, or, if they have transitioned, to use the facility of their corresponding gender.[6]

Perhaps even more encouraging, the Vancouver Catholic school board has approved policies to facilitate and accommodate transgender students.[7] The Catholic school board policy was created after a transgender girl complained, under the province's human rights legislation, that she was forced to use facilities designated for boys. She lived as a girl outside the school, and said that she became anxious and depressed whenever she was identified as a boy within the school.

Transitioning is in large part a public process, and it may not be possible to keep a student's transition private. As a result, it may be important for teachers and staff to be aware of a student's transgender identity. Transgender students should have the same ability as other students to discuss and express their gender identity and expression openly. When possible, the transgender student should control access to this information. School staff cannot be permitted to disclose a student's gender identity unless there is a legitimate reason to do so. Transgender students decide when, with whom, and how much of their private information is to be shared.

The intentional or constant refusal to respect and accommodate a student's gender identity or expression is a violation of human rights legislation.

ADULTS

Another aspect of the "mandatory" part of students' lives within the school community is their interaction with adults.

Whatever the actual content of courses or extracurricular activities, students are entitled to know that they are valued by their teachers and counsellors. Adults who are known to hold hostile views toward marginalized people and groups undermine that value and thus have no place in schools, nor do any groups run by such adults. This holds true even when these views might never be publicly expressed within the school or any related context.

ASSEMBLIES

Students also need to have facilitation of full inclusion and accommodation with respect to their experiences with "optional" school community activities. These include extracurricular activities and access to resources.

Extracurricular activities should not be predicated on identification with a particular religion or sexuality group. For example, it is well accepted that an annual December student assembly cannot be focused on Christmas. Otherwise, non-Christians would naturally feel like they were being othered.

Content, however, should not be excluded just because it reflects a majority sensibility such as Christianity. So long as students can offer content that involves the experiences of 2SLGBTQ+ students – which they should be able to do – they should also be able to include content that reflects a Christian experience.

Presumptions of sexuality (and religion) are manifested in various possible ways in extracurricular activities. If, for example, a school musical typically involves productions that underscore certain rigid gender norms or sexuality expectations, then certain students are always going to feel like they are "role-playing" – and not in a positive way – regardless of their involvement in the production.

In the context of religion, it may be that certain students may need space or time to participate in religious observances. They may require time and space to pray or to have access to certain types of food. Again, such accommodations should be made where feasible and in such ways that the students concerned are not singled out for scrutiny by their peers.

Students should not be escorted in or out of general activities while their fellow students look on. Students with special dietary requirements should not be served first or last or separately. Their religious practices should not necessarily be observed by other students, but they should also not be made to feel that their practices are required to be conducted out of view of others.

DANCES

The legal dispute that arose over Marc Hall's desire to bring his boyfriend to his school prom warrants further mention.[8] That controversy touches closely on an issue of facilitating optional activities that are accessible to all.

Justice MacKinnon allowed Marc Hall to attend the prom with his boyfriend for several reasons, including the court's conclusion that the prom was not an activity with religious significance. As a result, protection of religion was not of primary importance.

The school board not surprisingly defended its special position. The court, however, adopted an approach that avoided a hierarchy of constitutional protection – religion over 2SLGBTQ+ equality rights – facilitating space for all constitutional protections.

The court concluded that the constitutional protection of Catholic schools, found in section 93 of the *Constitution Act, 1867*, did not permit such schools to do as they pleased while ignoring other fundamental constitutional precepts. Religious protection had to be interpreted in light of other factors in society today, especially those values embodied in the constitution.

Furthermore, the court made this observation:

> In 1867, homosexual activity was viewed both as a crime and as a sickness. Today it is viewed as neither. Canadians' understanding of human behaviour and of its people has changed over the last 135 years.[9]
>
> ...
>
> The proper approach is to look at the rights as they existed in 1867 but then to apply 2002 common sense. In 2002, a School Board's legal authority (whether public or separate) is part of our provincial public educational system which is publicly funded by tax dollars and publicly regulated by the province.[10]

LIBRARIES

Optional aspects of school life relate to access to resources as well as participation in activities. Materials available in a school's library or at a counselling office should reflect the diversity that is possible in any school. Financial considerations might restrict the acquisition of such materials, but it should be remembered that many students who identify with or are part of marginalized communities are likely those most in need of such resources. Their needs should, therefore, be prioritized.

Students who are 2SLGBTQ+ should not have to make special requests for materials that make it awkward for them to have access. Some schools keep certain materials in the reserve section of their library or "behind the counter," or require special permission to access material online. Students may not be able to verbalize their needs or want to ask librarians or teachers for these resources, and they should not be expected to do so. Students are entitled to use whatever resources they require in a safe and accommodating space.

This balance may be difficult to achieve in some schools and may require that the same resources be made available in different ways or at different spaces.

PARENTAL APPROVAL

Access to resources of interest to 2SLGBTQ+ students should not depend upon parental approval or knowledge. Parents may well be hostile to such availability, and that disapproval will not be in the best interests of the students involved.

The Supreme Court of Canada has affirmed an inclusive accommodative ideal in Canadian law.[11] When the court ruled against the Surrey School District's objection to books depicting 2SLGBTQ+ parents, it underscored the importance of accommodating 2SLGBTQ+ students' needs in the face of religious opposition: "The School Act's emphasis on secularism reflects the fact that Canada is a diverse and multicultural society, bound together by the values of accommodation, tolerance and respect for diversity."[12]

Dr. Tourloukis, unhappy with 2SLGBTQ+ content in the lessons at his children's school, saw the issue – as frequently happens – as one of

2SLGBTQ+ rights versus religious accommodation. He took legal action because he claimed his parental authority over the education of his two children had been denied and his freedom of religion infringed.

His case lasted five years and was finally resolved in 2017 by the Ontario Court of Appeal. As often occurs in these sorts of disputes, the court concluded that Dr. Tourloukis's religious beliefs were sincere. The court readily accepted that Dr. Tourloukis believed he had an obligation to keep his children from being exposed to false teachings.

However, as we have seen, a sincere religious belief is not enough to prevail in the new climate, which favours 2SLGBTQ+ students.

The court imposes a burden on the person asserting their religious belief to provide objective evidence of infringement.[13] Once again, the law is clear – it is not enough just to claim that your rights have been infringed; you must prove it with evidence.

Schools that are reconfiguring their spaces to promote diversity and equity in order to accommodate 2SLGBTQ+ equality rights are winning these disputes.

The court had little difficulty in deciding that Dr. Tourloukis had not provided evidence that there had been any interference with or violation of his religious freedom or that of his children. Dr. Tourloukis had not established that his children were coerced into doing something that was contrary to his or their religious beliefs. He had not demonstrated that his children were prevented from manifesting or observing their own religious beliefs and practices. Finally, Dr. Tourloukis provided no objective evidence that the school board's policy[14] of promoting a climate that was inclusive and accepting of all pupils had in any way undermined his ability to transmit the precepts of his religion – including teachings about human sexuality – to his children.

STUDENT GROUPS AND CLUBS

An important part of a student's life relates to their own ability and right to establish school activities and groups that meet their individual needs. The importance of this has only increased as more and more students are becoming leaders of transformative activism within their schools. They should be able to establish, for example, a religion- or sexuality-based club in the same way that other students might be permitted to establish a photography group or a chess group.

If parental consent or involvement is not needed in the context of forming one group, it should not be needed in the forming of another.[15] In fact, some consideration might be given toward making it easier to establish certain groups.

In facilitating the inclusion of all, the inevitable stresses involved in student initiatives such as establishing GSAs or atheist groups should be acknowledged and accounted for. It can often be predicted, for example, that the establishment of certain groups might attract hostility or harassment from students' peers or others in the community. Therefore, consideration must be given to allowing students to use processes that are less fraught.

But it should not also be assumed that students want to be secretive or discreet about such groups. Such assumptions are just as problematic as assuming the usual processes must necessarily apply.

The right approach in these situations will often depend on the place and time when these efforts occur.

ADMINISTRATORS AND STAFF

Schools and school systems must facilitate inclusion and participation for adults as well. To date, there has been more actual implementation of this aspect of the facilitation issue than there has been for those involving students. This is because adults have been more willing to assert their rights than children and youth.[16]

That, of course, is changing.

In some cases, such as those involving teachers or other workers in schools, unions have played a large role in ensuring that adult voices are heard. It is for this reason that there is generally less "to be done" in this area.

While the insiders that should be facilitated in terms of their full membership in the school community are most obviously students and teachers, clearly the same approaches should be applied in the context of staff and administrators.

TEACHERS AS ROLE MODELS

Facilitation for teachers involves admission to a school's community from their first day in the school to their last.

Every teacher plays a role in the school community. They are the key figures in the practical school experience for students. Teachers are not only educators; they also have a legal duty to act as role models for their students. Legislation in each province and territory makes this clear.[17]

In *Attis v Board of Education of District 15 et al.*, the New Brunswick court, in the gender-exclusive language of the time, put the issue this way: "A teacher teaches. He is a role model. He also teaches by example. Children learn by example."[18]

Put simply, if a teacher is not fit to play the role of facilitator for all students in the ways discussed below then they are not fit to be a teacher in the new schools. Very often, characteristics of a teacher or counsellor, or their conduct relating to religion or sexuality – or both – have figured in claims that disqualify them for a specific role.

How does the law deal with a teacher who holds views hostile to marginalized groups and communities – views that have no place in schools? What if those views are not expressed in the school context but made known in other public ways?

School boards and the courts have a mixed track record in dealing with such situations.

LIMITS ON THE RIGHTS OF TEACHERS

Christopher Kempling[19] was a teacher/guidance counsellor in the Quesnel School District. He was suspended by the British Columbia College of Teachers and disciplined by his school district for discriminatory comments about gay people that he made in letters he wrote to the editor of a local newspaper.[20]

The dispute brought Kempling's right to freedom of expression into conflict with the equality rights of 2SLGBTQ+ students and staff. The Court of Appeal ruled that the limitations on Kempling's right to expression were justified by the school's duty to maintain a discrimination-free space. The case raised the issue of religious expression and what

• • • • • • •

KEY CASE
Kempling v British Columbia College of Teachers
2004 BCSC 133

The court held that non-discrimination is a core value of the public education system and that the integrity of that system was dependent upon teachers upholding that value by ensuring the school environment is accepting of all students.

In the case of a teacher making public homophobic and discriminatory comments, when such views are linked to their professional position as a teacher, harm to the integrity of the school system is an inevitable result.

• •

limitations exist for teachers wishing to tout their beliefs either to students or in a public manner.

Even though the Court of Appeal concluded that Kempling's freedom of expression, protected under section 2(b) of the *Charter*, had been infringed, the court also concluded that the infringement was justified under section 1 of the *Charter*.

Section 1 of the *Charter* confirms that the rights listed in the *Charter* are guaranteed. However, section 1 is also known as the "reasonable limits" clause because it permits the government to limit an individual's *Charter* rights when it is "demonstrably justified" to do so.

There were several reasons why the court preferred to find in favour of protecting the school from homophobic comments, weighing Mr. Kempling's freedom of expression against potentially limiting his rights.

First, the court expressed concern that his statements "damaged the integrity of the school system as a whole."[21] The court put the matter of balancing the expression rights of teachers against the effects their expression might have on the school in this way:

> This case rests in large part upon a resolution of how the competing *Charter* rights engaged are to be balanced. On the one

hand, lie the rights of Mr. Kempling to express his views concerning sexual morality which engage his s. 2(b) right to freedom of expression. On the other hand, lie the rights of homosexual students, and students in general, to a school environment that is free from discrimination and in harmony with s. 15 of the *Charter*. It is through the s. 1 analysis that these rights can be balanced.[22]

In addition, the court held that there had been undue harm caused due in part to Kempling's position as a teacher:

> As I have said, the harm in evidence in this case is not that of discriminatory actions directed against particular individuals, but rather is that sustained by the school system as a whole. In his writings, Mr. Kempling made clear that his discriminatory beliefs would inform his actions as a teacher and counsellor. His writings therefore, in themselves, undermine access to a discrimination-free education environment. Evidence that particular students no longer felt welcome within the school system, or that homosexual students refused to go to Mr. Kempling for counselling, is not required to establish that harm has been caused. Mr. Kempling's statements, even in the absence of any further actions, present an obstacle for homosexual students in accessing a discrimination-free education environment. These statements are therefore inherently harmful, not only because they deny access, but because in doing so they have damaged the integrity of the school system as a whole.[23]

In a similar case, Mr. Ross, a teacher, was ordered removed from the classroom by a Board of Inquiry for making anti-Semitic comments.[24] Ross had made public anti-Semitic writings and statements while he was off-duty. The local community clearly knew that the person making anti-Semitic comments (in his writings and through the media) was a well-known educator – even though Ross never signed his work as a teacher or linked his personal views to his professional rank.

The Supreme Court of Canada summed up Ross's position as a teacher in relation to his freedom of thought, belief, and opinion as follows:

In arguing that the [removal] order does infringe his freedom of religion, the respondent submits that the Act is being used as a sword to punish individuals for expressing their discriminating religious beliefs. He maintains that "[a]ll of the invective and hyperbole about anti-Semitism is really a smoke screen for imposing an officially sanctioned religious belief on society as a whole which is not the function of courts or Human Rights Tribunals in a free society." In this case, the respondent's freedom of religion is manifested in his writings, statements and publications. These, he argues, constitute "thoroughly honest religious statement[s]," and adds that it is not the role of this Court to decide what any particular religion believes.[25]

The Supreme Court also made some important comments about the position of teachers, generally.

Even though the court concluded that Ross's freedom of expression, protected under section 2(b) of the *Charter*, had been infringed, the

- - - - - - -

KEY CASE
Ross v New Brunswick School District No 15
[1996] 1 SCR 825

The Supreme Court affirmed that freedom of religion ensures that every individual must be free from government interference to hold and practise religious beliefs and opinions dictated by one's conscience. The importance of religious freedom is acknowledged; however, this right is not unlimited.

Religious freedom is restricted by the right of others to hold and to manifest beliefs and opinions of their own, and to be free from injury from the exercise of the freedom of religion of others. Freedom of religion is, therefore, subject to the limitations necessary to protect public safety, order, health, or morals, and the fundamental rights and freedoms of others.

court also concluded in this situation that the violation was demonstrably justified under section 1 of the *Charter*.

The court based its views partly on the likelihood that some views will have value in the pursuit of truth – surely an important goal in education.

The Supreme Court explained why racist speech was unlikely to promote the search of truth:

> This Court has held that there is very little chance that expression that promotes hatred against an identifiable group is true. Such expression silences the views of those in the target group and thereby hinders the free exchange of ideas feeding our search for political truth ... However, to give protection to views that attack and condemn the views, beliefs and practices of others is to undermine the principle that all views deserve equal protection and muzzles the voice of truth.[26]

The central conceit of teachers as role models is a recognition that teacher behaviour affects student behaviour. This had been accepted in *Ross*. When the behaviour of a teacher is on public display, that behaviour should not undermine the inclusive values of the school community. Whether or not particular deportment or speech occurs on school property is largely irrelevant.

As the unanimous Supreme Court explained:

> The conduct of a teacher is evaluated on the basis of his or her position, rather than whether the conduct occurs within the classroom or beyond ... teachers do not necessarily check their teaching hats at the school yard gate and may be perceived to be wearing their teaching hats even off duty.[27]
>
> ...
>
> It is on the basis of the position of trust and influence that we hold the teacher to high standards both on and off duty, and it is an erosion of these standards that may lead to a loss in the community of confidence in the public-school system.[28]

DISQUALIFYING TEACHERS

In the past, denominational or religion-based schools have frequently asserted their power to disqualify potential teachers on the basis of issues dealing with sexuality.[29]

At the same time, some religious persons have claimed that they cannot be disqualified from participation as teachers or counsellors in a public school on the basis of their discriminatory views about sexuality.[30]

There need to be, of course, some occasions on which matters of religion and sexuality will disqualify a person from being a teacher or counsellor in either a denominational or public school.

But when?

The inclusion, accommodation, and facilitation of membership in a school's community for all – but especially for the students – must be the main focus. While this issue should, therefore, be determined primarily from the perspective of potential students, the context of other colleagues or outsider adults who might interact with the school community should also be considered.

A person should be included no matter their religion or sexuality, unless their inclusion impedes others – especially students – in their ability to experience a sense of security, inclusion, or full citizenship in the school community. If a teacher or counsellor has done something or expressed views that indicate that they would be averse to or even hostile toward practical equality for others at their school, then there is legal justification not to accept that person into the school community.

If the teacher or counsellor simply maintains views or characteristics that are not consistent with the message of the school system, that alone should not be enough to exclude the person or to result in discipline subsequent to hiring.

There is a difference between holding beliefs and acting upon them. That is the difference between thought and discriminatory conduct. The distinction comes down to the process of gaining credentials as a teacher or counsellor and in using or maintaining those credentials once gained. If in any of those contexts a teacher or counsellor voices or shows support for exclusionary policies or practices, then the teacher or counsellor should be considered to have lost or not attained sufficient credibility as a teacher.

If a teacher attends a church where homophobic or racist views are expressed, then that alone may not be sufficient. If they have forbidden their own children from visiting a synagogue for whatever reason, that also would not usually be enough to raise concerns about their efficacy as a teacher.

DENOMINATIONAL SCHOOLS

If a teacher supported a covenant that was homophobic, racist, or otherwise discriminatory as part of their education in becoming a teacher, it should in turn be appropriate for the governing body of teachers to require at least that the teacher receive professional human rights and anti-discriminatory practices training before working with children and youth. This sort of assessment can be made even in the context of a constitutionally protected denominational or religious school system.

If a would-be or working teacher or guidance counsellor holds personal views or practices in their life outside of school that are not consistent with the denominational teachings of the school, there is no reason why that person should be thought unfit to be part of the school's community. There is no presumptive reason to imagine that said teacher will not translate the views or values of the school into the education system.

If, however, a teacher working at a denominational school were to publicly write or speak against the Catholic Church, then the Catholic denominational school system would be entitled to reject that teacher from its community.

Unfortunately, past cases have overreached in terms of protection for a denomination's exclusionary powers. In one such case, a school board was permitted to enforce a policy to exclude teachers whose personal lives did not conform with the board's stated religious values.

In 1984, the Supreme Court was asked to consider a policy at a Catholic school requiring teachers to conform strictly with the teachings of the Catholic Church.[31] The school terminated a teacher, Ms.

Caldwell, because she had married a divorced man in a civil ceremony, contrary to Church doctrine. The school's requirement that its teachers observe strict religious adherence was justified by the court on the ground that the school's purpose was to instill principles of Catholicism in students.[32]

Such an approach is overbroad today.

First, as the Marc Hall prom case illustrated,[33] there are a number of aspects inherent to a denominational school's operation that might *not* be subject to protection in relation to religion-based claims. Also, it should be noted that *Caldwell* is a pre-*Charter* case. Though introduced in 1982, the *Charter's* equality provisions did not come into effect until 1985. As such, the decision made does not reflect the legal recognition of sexual orientation rights that have been accepted in other contexts.

Caldwell can be acknowledged, but it is very likely on shaky legal ground in a modern context.

RESPONSIBLE ACCOMMODATION

Accommodation for teachers should not mean that students will bear the consequences of another person's religious views. Common spaces should not be segregated to accommodate divisive religious views.

Activities for teachers and other adults in schools should not be organized on the basis that everybody shares a particular sexuality or religion – even in denominational schools. It should not be assumed that everyone celebrates Christmas, for example – although there is no reason why Christmas could not be marked or celebrated in an inclusive community.

If weddings are celebrated, same-sex weddings should also be marked as causes for celebration. And it should be acknowledged that 2SLGBTQ+ couples have children, and that heterosexual students often have 2SLGBTQ+ parents. There might also be increased accommodation made for certain religious practices for staff members who do not interact exclusively with students. For example, it is easier to accommodate the religious needs of a person working in a school's office whose faith requires her to cover her face than it would be if she were a teacher or counsellor.

It is also possible that such a person, depending on the position, might be afforded greater scope for expressing discriminatory views outside of their school. However, the impact of such expression or actions on adults as well as children should be kept in mind when making that decision.

OUTSIDERS

The school community is not a closed community.

It is not confined to its students, teachers, and administrators. All individuals and groups have interests in the educational system of their respective communities. There is no reason why anyone should not be given appropriate and equal access to this facet of their community.

This access must be carried out with respect both to the school community – including information and activities provided in schools – and to the physical facilities when being used by outsiders. Facilitation, of course, does not mean that outsiders will have the same level of access and inclusion that would apply to school insiders – except perhaps in after-hours matters when the usual insiders are not there.

There are of course good reasons to protect insiders, especially students, from outsiders and outside information. This can be as much a matter of physical safety as it is the privacy of students and staff.

Some groups and individuals have traditionally been given such access to schools. Religion-based groups, especially those whose backgrounds are rooted in more widespread, traditional religions, have made their voices heard in the educational system. Many, of course, run their own denominational schools, usually with state accreditation and financial support. Others make their voices heard in the public school system either directly or indirectly – such as with the *Chamberlain* case.[34]

Some groups enter the public school system in a more direct way, supplying information and services to students. This is generally positive; however, that access should not be achieved in any manner that associates part of the school community with the views or perspectives of the outsiders.

For example, in Edmonton, the public school board decided to discontinue the involvement of the Edmonton Pregnancy Care Centre in presenting workshops as part of the school's mandatory sexual education curriculum.[35] The Edmonton Pregnancy Care Centre had a faith background and advocated for abstinence as a preferred method of sexual health and birth control. While the Centre said it did not present religious views in its sessions, there was concern from some parents about the involvement of the group. Parents were particularly concerned with the possibility that the Centre would present health information grounded in religious ideology within a mandatory course intended for all students.

2SLGBTQ+ OUTSIDER GROUPS

In the past, outside groups and individuals associated with 2SLGBTQ+ issues have been frequently excluded – or at least not actively included – from schools.

Because of the preconception that such sexualities are corrupting influences and not normal in children, such groups and individuals have been kept away. And due to the fact that 2SLGBTQ+ people have been long prohibited from adopting and discouraged from having children, there has long been a preconception that the school community is prohibited or irrelevant to them.

But 2SLGBTQ+ people do have children, and heterosexual children do have 2SLGBTQ+ parents. Additionally, heterosexual parents obviously have 2SLGBTQ+ children who could themselves benefit from experiencing the viewpoints of 2SLGBTQ+ outsiders and groups.

In Ontario, T.E.A.C.H. (Teens Educating and Confronting Homophobia) is a volunteer organization in which 2SLGBTQ+ teenagers make themselves available to come and speak in schools. The organization employs anti-oppression education to deliver anti-homophobia workshops in high schools. Teenage peer facilitators lead workshops that encourage students to think critically about homophobia and heterosexism in their communities.

Efforts to encourage and facilitate the in-school involvement of groups such as T.E.A.C.H. as well as individuals who can speak to 2SLGBTQ+ issues should occur at levels equivalent to other individual and outsider groups who are routinely welcomed.

A MESSAGE WORTH REPEATING

At the end of the day, Dr. Tourloukis received the same message from the Ontario Court of Appeal as others who had made similar religion-based arguments to the Supreme Court of Canada.

Exposing children attending non-denominational public schools to ideas that challenge or even contradict the sincerely held religious beliefs of their parents does not amount to an infringement of religious freedom.[36]

Allowing some students to remove themselves on a regular basis from class discussions promoting diversity, inclusion, and acceptance – as part of a larger program intended to promote those same values – would "run a serious risk of endorsing the non-acceptance of students of other family backgrounds, sexual orientations, gender expressions and gender identities."[37]

Schools, then, are free to utilize, and to permit others access to, school spaces in order to promote diversity, and the law supports that right in the face of religious-based objections.

The message is clear. Like any other *Charter* right, the protection of freedom of religion must be measured in relation to other rights. Requiring public school students to acquire an awareness of Canada's diverse realities is not a substantial infringement of freedom of religion.

CONCLUSION

Getting There

TWO CURRICULUMS

The *Canadian Oxford Dictionary* defines curriculum as a collection of subjects taught.

Looking below the surface, curriculum is not just about facts, numbers, and knowledge. It is also about beliefs and values. Curriculum plays a central role in shaping how students approach and consider questions of sexual and religious diversity – and everything else.

In a general sense, curriculum is about *what gets taught in schools*.

The teaching of prepared, fixed, and programmed content is associated with a specific grade and specific subjects or courses.

This is the formal or official curriculum.[1]

The science syllabus, the mathematics or social studies outline are part of the official curriculum. Add in geography, history, English, music, physical education, and other subjects, and the official curriculum of *what gets taught* takes shape.

OFFICIAL CURRICULUM

The lessons of the official curriculum are the formal teachings of a school. Sometimes referred to as the formal or manifest curriculum, the official curriculum includes all of the readily identifiable subjects such as geography, history, and English.

Co-existing with the formal curriculum, scholars have identified an informal or hidden curriculum.[2] This hidden curriculum transmits social meanings and promotes cultural outcomes through schooling practices and activities that occur within schools. The hidden curriculum includes what students learn from being at school apart from the stated educational objectives of schools.[3]

The hidden curriculum contains implicit and explicit messages that refer to both behaviour and values. Its concept recognizes two crucial consequences of what it means to go to school.

First, the hidden curriculum acknowledges that the outcomes of schooling are not limited to the communication of knowledge required in the approved, official curriculum.

Second, accepting that there is a hidden curriculum of messaging and learning being conveyed to students means conceding that schools are also not neutral conveyers of knowledge and information.

In terms of conduct, "much of what happens in schools has to do with the influencing of behaviour rather than with the learning of prescribed content or skills."[4]

Historically, the voices and stories of 2SLGBTQ+ students have been marginalized, demonized, or rendered completely invisible in the official curriculum of schools. Acting "straight" and rejecting anything

● ● ● ● ● ● ● ● ● ● ● ● ●

HIDDEN CURRICULUM

The hidden curriculum refers to the values and norms that students learn in the hallways, in the schoolyard, and at other places around the school – including the classroom – that are not part of the official, prescribed curriculum. While not found in any syllabus or on any course outline, the hidden curriculum refers to the lessons students learn just by going to school day after day, year after year.

The hidden curriculum reinforces identities, promotes cultural outcomes, and reinforces power structures. The hidden curriculum includes all informal interaction among students (and teachers) and teaches students how the world – and they – should be.

● ●

other than straightness has been the historical norm in the formal curriculum.

Recognizing and valuing sexual and gender difference has often been absent from the books and materials used in schools. Curriculum designers have failed to attach worth, meaning, and legitimacy to the lives of 2SLGBTQ+ students, who do not see themselves or their realities reflected in class.

However, what the concept of the hidden curriculum tells us is that there are two fronts on which students are learning about what it means to be 2SLGBTQ+. The hidden curriculum is insidious because it is, for the most part, unacknowledged. Nonetheless, the lessons of the hidden curriculum begin in kindergarten and continue throughout the early grades and through to high school.

And yet if there is any content at all that addresses 2SLGBTQ+ lives, it is often scattered, limited, and offered from the perspective that 2SLGBTQ+ lives are a "problem" to be "dealt with." Also absent are any attempts to address the multiple spheres of identity that intersectionality asks us to consider, and the need to move past one-dimensional approaches to diversity, inclusion, and celebration.

Even when this kind of topical approach to 2SLGBTQ+ lives does occur in a formal curriculum, it usually is not offered until students are older – years after they first encounter the marginalizing and culturally sidelining effects of the hidden curriculum.

SCHOOL CLIMATE

One does not have to imagine the negative lessons of the hidden curriculum or the hostile school climate it produces for 2SLGBTQ+ students. Studies confirm the constant denigration of 2SLGBTQ+ students in schools, the hateful language 2SLGBTQ+ students hear every day, and the harassment and abusive conduct to which they are often subjected.[5]

Research has found that most 2SLGBTQ+ students face homophobia and transphobia every day. And often their experience includes schools doing little to change an existing hostile school climate.[6]

Too often, 2SLGBTQ+ students experience schools where the official curriculum may celebrate diversity but the curriculum of the hallway sends a different message. In many ways, 2SLGBTQ+ students and their heterosexual peers receive the not-so-quiet message that 2SLGBTQ+ students are objects of contempt to whom human rights do not apply.[7]

It is impossible for 2SLGBTQ+ students to articulate their own identities in high schools that fail to acknowledge them. The mere experience of going to school creates a hierarchy in which the higher status of heterosexual students is persistently vouched for while sexual- and gender-minority voices are consistently discouraged and stifled.[8]

Adhering to conceptions of safety as "security" or "control," and restricting discussions of safe schools to conversations about how to contain only the threat of physical violence, has led policy makers to ignore or undervalue the ways in which gender scripts and heteronormative privilege make schools less safe for 2SLGBTQ+ students. This is particularly frustrating for 2SLGBTQ+ students and their allies who consistently define safety in terms of inclusiveness.[9]

All of this occurs, of course, to the detriment of sexual-minority youth who are not only devalued but also threatened in ways that are not being considered under current approaches.

THE THIRD CURRICULUM

School safety cannot be achieved merely by punishing bullies who torment 2SLGBTQ+ students. Safety must be approached in terms of equity and social justice in order to create school climates where 2SLGBTQ+ students can enjoy the dignity of full citizenship and participation in everyday life within their community.

Education that is 2SLGBTQ+ inclusive improves school climates for all students, yes, but especially for 2SLGBTQ+ students, students with sexual- and gender-minority parents, and any student who is negatively impacted by homophobic, transphobic, heteronormative school climates.[10]

Parents, legislators, educators, and administrators are recognizing the need to ensure 2SLGBTQ+ safety and inclusion in Canadian schools. The individual provinces and territories have exclusive jurisdiction over education within their borders, meaning that the approach to 2SLGBTQ+-inclusive education has not been uniform.

Though there have been significant, but varying, developments made across the country, we have observed that Ontario, Manitoba, and Alberta remain the only provinces to mandate, through legislation, students' right to establish a GSA. More is needed at the levels of research and capacity-building within the educational community if public and denominational schools are to be transformed into places that are inclusive of all forms of diversity in Canada, including gender and sexual diversity.

Education that is 2SLGBTQ+-inclusive strives to make schools safe and inclusive places for both 2SLGBTQ+ and heterosexual students alike – like Azmi Jubran and others – who are directly targeted, or otherwise distressed, by harassment and marginalization on the basis of gender and sexuality.[11]

While the need to make a difference in transforming school climate is broadly recognized by Canadian educators and significant progress has been made in some jurisdictions – the law is increasingly supportive – some stakeholders remain reluctant to act.[12] But if transformative action is to occur, creating safe spaces for 2SLGBTQ+ students in both public and denominational schools Canada-wide, educative practices aimed at transforming the larger heteronormative climate of schools are required.

Finally, the following suggestions may help point the way toward the necessary transformation. These suggestions must be met if 2SLGBTQ+ youth are to receive safe and equal access to education.

Teachers and administrators must recognize that current conceptions of safety are insufficiently robust and must be re-conceptualized so that inclusion, equity, and social justice are accepted as necessary parts of school safety.

Principals in each province are responsible for ensuring the approved curriculum is taught in all classrooms. Saskatchewan's *Education Act*, for example, states that principals must "organize the program of courses and instruction approved by the board of education ..."[13]

School administrators can show curricular leadership by embracing the ideals of inclusion and accommodation at the school level. Principals and vice-principals can do this by supporting 2SLGBTQ+ students and teachers, and guaranteeing that they are free from harassment and are in a safe and caring environment. This teaches students and others about the informal curriculum, namely what is and is not acceptable in terms of appropriate behaviour.

School administrators can also support teachers and students who wish to examine issues surrounding sexuality and gender in the curriculum in an appropriate and professional manner. This entails ensuring that suitable 2SLGBTQ+-friendly curricula are available in the school and that opportunities for in-classroom discussion of these materials are permitted and encouraged.

School leaders must also, for example, support the establishment and promotion of gay-straight alliances as sites of affirmation and celebration for 2SLGBTQ+ students. Too often this burden falls on the shoulders of the students themselves.

Principals and vice-principals can stand up to political pressures from those few irate and intolerant parents and community members who wish to keep curricular materials about 2SLGBTQ+ students out of the schools. By creating a safe curricular space, they effectively are saying no to harmful attitudes and are assisting in legitimizing the place of sexual minorities in schools.

At the school level, administrators and teachers have an especially important role to play as role models who embody the lived curriculum. Students are watching and consciously or unconsciously looking for guidance about how to treat themselves and other people.

Education that is 2SLGBTQ+-inclusive, however, must do *more* than include. Privilege must be implicated, understood, and accounted for. Inclusion alone merely sustains oppression and threatens the safety of 2SLGBTQ+ students. Inclusive education alone does little to address systemic power imbalances and oppression.

Heterosexual students must be implicated in school processes and the regimes of silence, invisibility, and oppression inherent within the official and unofficial curricula and general school climate. Curriculum content must not be merely a presentation of information about 2SLGBTQ+ students, received by heterosexual students from their distanced and normative positions.

A curriculum that fails to address these issues allows cisgender and heterosexual students to remain free from responsibility with respect to the very cultural practices and processes that invariably lead to the harassment of 2SLGBTQ+ students, so long as the only culpability that remains is for landing a physical blow or hurling an insult. So long as safety is limited to incidents that occur between two individuals, and so long as the victimizer alone is permitted to bear responsibility – and not the larger culture that has produced them – 2SLGBTQ+ students will never be safe.

There is another, critical way in which inclusive education alone is inadequate.

The curriculum and the general life of the school must not just include but also *celebrate* 2SLGBTQ+ youth – and friendships between heterosexual and 2SLGBTQ+ students. As the law has progressed to accept new possibilities, so, too, have we moved away from mere – and offensive – notions of "tolerance." Students who are 2SLGBTQ+ and 2SLGBTQ+ parents must be included, yes, but also embraced and celebrated.

A 2SLGBTQ+-inclusive curriculum must be widespread and mandatory, and originate at the ministerial level. Otherwise, teachers will not implement 2SLGBTQ+ content in an official curriculum, nor will transformative possibilities be achievable.

A 2SLGBTQ+-inclusive curriculum must also begin in the early grades and in all social spaces of schools (i.e., as early as kindergarten or Grade 1). The hidden curriculum begins its insidious work very early. To parents and educators who say some children are too young to hear of different sexualities and identities, we say, "they are already hearing about them." And in negative ways.

The official curriculum must catch up to and counteract what the hidden curriculum is already hard at work promoting. To those who still object, it is important to bear in mind that one of the nefarious ways that homophobia and transphobia operate is through inaction in the face of need.

A JOURNEY FOR EVERYONE

The outcomes of the hidden curriculum are likely to land more securely in the minds of students than arithmetic, and be more effective than the official curriculum, generally.

The lessons taught by the official curriculum are heeded and remembered, and experienced daily.[14] Because these lessons are stable, pervasive, and consistent over the many years that students attend school, the need for 2SLGBTQ+-inclusive education to counter such well-entrenched hostility, beginning in the early grades, is clear.

In this sense, a 2SLGBTQ+-inclusive curriculum is a third curriculum, a transformation of the current official curriculum that – unless specific efforts in specific schools have been made – at the very least fails to acknowledge 2SLGBTQ+ students or parents.

And certainly, 2SLGBTQ+-inclusive education can be seen as operating against the invidious (and discriminatory) functioning of the hidden curriculum that has consistently denigrated 2SLGBTQ+ students and persons over many years.

Widely, 2SLGBTQ+ students characterize the threats to their safety as "expected," "inevitable," and "encouraged" by a heteronormative school culture that promotes a hierarchy of gender and sexuality. Make no mistake, heteronormativity impacts all trans students and students of marginalized sexualities. In this hierarchy, students monitor their own behaviours and presentation, and those of their peers for signs of "difference" and "otherness" – is he gay? In this way, the norms of both gender and sexuality are under constant surveillance, and transgressions may be enforced with looks, words, or physical force.

That is how the hidden curriculum works – over time and years, and throughout the life of every student.

However, the law has changed dramatically in recent years in terms of what it means to be 2SLGBTQ+ in Canadian society and, in particular, in schools. In 1995, the Supreme Court of Canada recognized sexual orientation as a protected category in the *Charter*. And in 2004, less than ten years later, same-sex marriage was legalized throughout the entire country.

Around these cultural sign posts, courts have been faced with more and more cases in which the assertion of 2SLGBTQ+ rights, and the right to be free from discrimination, have been met with opposition by those who feel that granting equality to 2SLGBTQ+ persons and students means an infringement of their religious beliefs, practices, and rights.

In resolving these conflicts, the courts have been faced with a balancing act. In many cases, in different contexts, they have favoured the protection and equality of 2SLGBTQ+ persons – and students – over the insignificant or even imagined infringement of religion-based rights claims.

The power of the law is on the right side in this. Gabriel Picard and Azmi Jubran contributed, heroically, to that power.

Gabriel Picard said something simple and at the same time monumental. He began his human rights action against his school board "to change a culture."

His principal told him that changing a culture was "impossible."

The suggestions offered here for a new curriculum, with the law on board, point the way to just that kind of monumental change, offering support for and evidence that transforming schools is *not* impossible.

It is *possible*. Students, teachers, and some legislators are leading the way.

But transformation requires resources. Teachers must have the philosophical and financial support of their school board, their school's administration, and the support of colleagues.

Change is, for 2SLGBTQ+ students, the new inevitable.

For some schools, that change has already arrived. Students who are 2SLGBTQ+ are not only recognized and included, they are celebrated.

New schools. New students.

For other schools, the goal of creating safe, equitable, and inclusive places for 2SLGBTQ+ students may be more long-term.

That is no reason not to start now.

It is a journey for everyone.

Notes

INTRODUCTION: JOURNEYS

1 Elizabeth A. McConnell, Michelle Birkett, and Brian Mustanski, "Families Matter: Social Support and Mental Health Trajectories among Lesbian, Gay, Bisexual and Transgender Youth," *Journal of Adolescent Health* 59, 6 (2016): 674.
2 Steven T. Russell, Joseph Kosciw, Stacey Horn, and Elizabeth Saewyc, "Social Policy Report: Safe Schools Policy for LGBTQ Students," *Sharing Child and Youth Development Knowledge*, 24 (2010): 4.
3 Stephen T. Russell and Stacey S. Horn, *Sexual Orientation, Gender Identity, and Schooling: The Nexus of Research, Practice, and Policy* (Oxford: Oxford University Press, 2017).
4 See Donn Short, *Don't Be So Gay: Queers, Bullying and Making Schools Safe* (Vancouver: UBC Press, 2013); Short, *Am I Safe Here? LGBTQ Teens and Bullying* (Vancouver: On Point Press, 2017). See also Gerald Walton, "Bullying and Homophobia in Canadian Schools: The Politics of Policies, Programs and Educational Leadership," *Journal of Gay and Lesbian Issues in Education* 1, 4 (2003): 23–36; Walton, "The Notion of Bullying through the Lens of Foucault and Critical Theory," *Journal of Educational Thought* 39, 1 (2005): 55; Walton, "Bullying Widespread: A Critical Analysis of Research and Public Discourse on Bullying," *Journal of School Violence* 4, 1 (2005): 91.
5 K.W. Crenshaw, "Mapping the Margins: Intersectionality, Identity Politics, and Violence against Women of Color," *Stanford Law Review* 43, 6 (1991): 1241.
6 A.D. Zongrone, N.L. Truong, and J.G. Kosciw, *Erasure and Resilience: The Experiences of LGBTQ Students of Color, Native and Indigenous LGBTQ Youth in U.S. Schools* (New York: GLSEN, 2020), xvi.
7 Ibid.
8 Zongrone, Introduction, note 6, xx.
9 Ibid.
10 *Canadian Charter of Rights and Freedoms, Part 1 of the Constitution Act, 1982*, being Schedule B to the Canada Act 1982 (UK), 1982, c 11 [*Charter*]. See also *Reference re: Same-Sex Marriage*, 2004 SCC 79 [*Reference*], paras 50–52.

11 See *Reference*, ibid.; see also *Dagenais v Canadian Broadcasting Corp*, [1994] 3 SCR 835 [*Dagenais*]; *R v Mentuck*, 2001 SCC 76; *R v NS*, 2012 SCC 72 [*NS*]; *Law Society of British Columbia v Trinity Western University*, 2018 SCC 32 [*LSBC v TWU*].
12 See *NS*, ibid.
13 In this book, "sexuality" includes both sexual orientation and the expression of sexuality. Sexual orientation refers to an individual's sexual, psychological, and emotional feelings of attraction to others. We acknowledge and support that more and more legal challenges have been and will continue to be based upon identities not grounded in sexuality.
14 In this book, "religion" means a set of spiritual beliefs, typically based on "faith" rather than reason or evidence, and includes the practices associated with those beliefs. In practice, religion involves a person's attachment to a structured organization that serves as a focal point for those who share said beliefs. In law, a religious belief is a sincerely held belief whether or not that belief is also held by co-religionists.
15 *LSBC v TWU*, Introduction, note 11.
16 "Manitoba Human Rights Commission to Hear Transgender Girl's Case in July," *CBC*. January 12, 2016. <https://www.cbc.ca/news/canada/manitoba/manitoba-human-rights-commission-to-hear-transgender-girl-s-case> [perma.cc/5JVV-5PUG].
17 "Bella's Family Reaches Transgender-Rights Settlement with School Division," *Winnipeg Sun*. March 11, 2016. <https://winnipegsun.com/2016/03/11/bellas-family-reaches-transgender-rights-settlement-with-school-division> [perma.cc/M596-WCQF].
18 Danelle Cloutier, "Transgender Girl's Human Rights Complaint against School Division in Winnipeg Resolved," *CBC*. March 11, 2016. <www.cbc.ca/news> [perma.cc/PF9W-DH8Q].
19 Ibid.

CHAPTER 1: LEGAL POSSIBILITIES

1 See *Bill 18, The Public Schools Amendment Act (Safe and Inclusive Schools)*, 2nd Sess, 40th Leg, Manitoba, 2013 [*Bill 18*]. See Short, "Bound for Glory: Bill 18, The Public Schools Amendment Act (Safe and Inclusive Schools)," *Manitoba Law Journal* 36, 2 (2013): 115.
2 See Gerald Walton, Introduction, note 4; see also Short, *Don't Be So Gay!* and Short, *Am I Safe Here?* Introduction, note 4. See also Short, "Queering Schools, GSAs and the Law," *The Gay Agenda: Claiming Space, Identity & Justice*, edited by Gerald Walton, 327–43 (New York: Peter Lang, 2014).
3 Nick Martin, "Steinbach *Bill 18*," *Winnipeg Free Press*, March 7, 2013. <www.winnipegfreepress.com> [perma.cc/98AA-VUMC].
4 See Matthew Coutts, "Manitoba Christian School Opposes Anti-Bullying Law Protecting Homosexual Clubs," *Daily Brew*. February 26, 2013. <ca.news.yahoo.com> [perma.cc/49Q3-KP7Y].
5 Thadeus Batlinski, "Manitoba Anti-Bullying Bill 18 May Force Gay-Straight Alliance Clubs on Independent Religious School," *Lifesite News*. March 1, 2013. <www.lifesitenews.com/news/manitoba-anti-bullying-bill-18-may-force-gay-straight-alliance-clubs-on-ind> [perma.cc/L2ET-UG5K].
6 Josh Wingrove, "Gay Teen Holds the Line for Manitoba Bullying Bill," *Globe and Mail*. March 17, 2013. <www.theglobeandmail.com> [perma.cc/V7R9-4KYM].

7 "GSA Told Not to Advertise: Student. School Board Accused of Discrimination," *Winnipeg Free Press*. March 1, 2013. <www.winnipegfreepress.com/local/gsa-told-not-to-advertise-student-194137041.html> [perma.cc/QU8Z-8BX4].
8 *Charter*, Introduction, note 10, ss 2(a), 15.
9 See *Egan v Canada*, [1995] 2 SCR 513, 124 DLR (4th) 609 [*Egan*].
10 See e.g., *Human Rights Code*, RSO 1990, c H.19, s 2(2).
11 *The Saskatchewan Human Rights Code*, 2018, SS 2018, c S-24.2, s 13(1).
12 Ibid., s 2(1).
13 *R v Big M Drug Mart*, [1985] 1 SCR 295 [*Big M*].
14 Ibid., para 94.
15 *Trinity Western University v British Columbia College of Teachers*, 2001 SCC 31, para 36, [2001] 1 SCR 772 [*TWU v BCCT*].
16 *Big M*, Chapter 1, note 13, para 95.
17 *R v Crawford*, [1995] 1 SCR 858, para 34. See also *LSBC v TWU*, Introduction, note 11.
18 *Dagenais*, Introduction, note 11, para 72.
19 *Egan*, Chapter 1, note 9.
20 *Vriend v Alberta*, [1998] 1 SCR 493 [*Vriend*].
21 *Charter*, Introduction, note 10, s 15(1). See also ibid.
22 *Bill 13, An Act to Amend the Education Act with Respect to Bullying and Other Matters*, 1st Sess, 40th Leg, Ontario (assented to June 19, 2012), SO 2012, c 5 [*Bill 13*].
23 *Reference*, Introduction, note 10.
24 Ibid.
25 *Syndicat Northcrest v Amselem*, 2004 SCC 47 [*Amselem*]; see also *SL v Commission scolaire des Chênes*, 2012 SCC 7 [*SL v Commission*]. See also *Loyola High School v Quebec (Attorney General)*, 2015 SCC 12; and *LSBC v TWU*, Introduction, note 11.
26 *Amselem*, ibid., para 46.
27 *Ross v New Brunswick School District No 15*, [1996] 1 SCR 825 [*Ross*].
28 *SL v Commission*, Chapter 1, note 25, para 32.
29 *Amselem*, Chapter 1, note 25, para 59.
30 *Reference*, Introduction, note 10.
31 *Saskatchewan (Human Rights Commission) v Whatcott*, 2013 SCC 11.
32 See Short, *Don't Be So Gay!* and *Am I Safe Here?* Introduction, note 4. See also Bruce MacDougall, *Queer Judgments: Homosexuality, Expression and the Courts in Canada* (Toronto: UTP, 2000), 98.
33 For example, s 93, *The Constitution Act*, restricts the Ontario legislature from making certain laws that infringe upon certain interests of Roman Catholic schools. However, the rights that are protected are those rights that existed in 1867 and – as the Supreme Court has said, and we mentioned in Chapter 1 and again, here – no rights are absolute.
34 Even more surprisingly, there were no legal challenges with respect to the equivalent proposals in Ontario with regard to that province's *Bill 13*. In Ontario, Roman Catholic schools have constitutional protections that schools in Manitoba do not have. However, notwithstanding these protections, Roman Catholic school trustees and administrators may be fearful that the legal tide has turned against their opposition to 2SLGBTQ+ rights and inclusion.

35 *LSBC v TWU*, Introduction, note 11; *Trinity Western University v Law Society of Upper Canada*, 2018 SCC 33.
36 Elizabeth Myer, Tracey Peter, Janice Ristock, and Catherine Taylor, "Conflicting Beliefs, Perceptions and Behaviors." In "Special Issue on International Perspectives on Homophobic and Transphobic Bullying in Schools," ed. Joe Kosciw and Oren Pizmony-Levy, *Journal of LGBT Youth* 13, 1–2 (2016): 112–40.
37 Flavio Nienow, "Schools in Rural Areas Lack Support for 2SLGBTQ+ Students," *Shellbrook Chronicle*. May 23, 2014. <shellbrookchronicle.com> [perma.cc/DDY6-867C].
38 Ontario Catholic Schools Trustees' Association, "'Respecting Difference': A Resource for Catholic Schools in the Province of Ontario," *Diocese of London*. January 25, 2012. <dol.ca> [perma.cc/5RQB-BV36].
39 Ibid.
40 This judgment relies on a passage from: Franjo Cardinal Seper, "Persona Humana: Declaration on Certain Questions Concerning Sexual Ethics," *Vatican*. December 29, 1975. <www.vatican.va> [perma.cc/KUN3-EVQF], viii. "In Sacred Scripture [homosexual relations] are condemned as a serious depravity and even presented as the sad consequence of rejecting God. This judgment of Scripture does not of course permit us to conclude that all those who suffer from this anomaly are personally responsible for it, but it does attest to the fact that homosexual acts are intrinsically disordered and can in no case be approved of."
41 Canadian Press, "Human Rights Complaint Prompts New Gender Policy in Vancouver Catholic Schools," *CBC*. July 16, 2014. <www.cbc.ca/> [perma.cc/MK63-3F6K].
42 Ibid.
43 Ibid.
44 "Sexual Orientation – Principles," *The Evangelical Fellowship of Canada*. Accessed July 12, 2019. <bbnc.evangelicalfellowship.ca> [perma.cc/P3NC-AKGT].
45 See Tonya Callaghan, *That's So Gay: Homosexuality in Canadian Catholic Schools* (Saarbrucken: AV Akademikerverlag, 2012); and Tonya Callaghan, *Heterosexism and Transphobia in Canadian Catholic Schools* (Toronto: UTP, 2018).
46 See Short, *Don't Be So Gay!* Introduction, note 4. See also MacDougall and Short, "Religion-Based Claims for Impinging on Queer Citizenship," *Dalhousie Law Journal* 33, 2 (2010): 133.
47 For the international level, see *Convention on the Rights of the Child*, GA Res 44/25, UNGAOR, 44th Sess, Supp No 49, UN Doc A/44/49 (1989) 166.
48 Regina Board of Education SD No. 4, "Regina Public Schools Board Policy 1 – Division Foundational Statements." Last modified May 28, 2019. <www.reginapublicschools.ca/board_policies> [perma.cc/YH8H-7TTU].
49 Alex Abramovich, "No Fixed Address: Young, Queer, and Restless," *Youth Homelessness in Canada: Implications for Policy and Practice*, edited by Stephen Gaetz, Bill O'Grady, et al. (Toronto: COH, 2017), 387.
50 See Catherine Taylor, Tracey Peter, Christopher Campbell, Elizabeth Meyer, Janice Ristock, and Donn Short, *The Every Teacher Project on LGBTQ-Inclusive Education in Canada's K-12 Schools* (Winnipeg: Manitoba Teachers' Society, 2015), 60–65.
51 Grant Burr, "Wiens Wins $70,000 Scholarship," *The Carillon*. May 29, 2014. <www.winnipegfreepress.com> [perma.cc/SM4U-3Z6T].

Notes to pages 43–65

52 Kim Kaschor, "Diversity Policy Needs Update, Says Manitoba 2SLGBTQ+ Advocate Evan Wiens," *CBC*. April 25, 2016. <www.cbc.ca/news/canada/manitoba/diversity-policy-needs-update-says-manitoba-LGBTQ-advocate-evan-wiens-1.3549776> [perma.cc/K7XC-HCH8].
53 Ibid.
54 Ibid.
55 Ibid.

CHAPTER 2: THE SAFE AND WELCOMING SCHOOL

1 See Taylor et al., *The Every Teacher Project*, Chapter 1, note 50, 39.
2 See Short, *Don't Be So Gay!* and *Am I Safe Here?* Introduction, note 4.
3 Donn Short, "Safe Schools: The Threat from Within?" (2011) 51: 3, *EdCan Network*.
4 Peter McLaren, "Critical Pedagogy: A Look at the Major Concepts," *The Critical Pedagogy Reader*, 2nd ed., edited by Antonia Darder, Marta P. Baltodano, and Rodolfo D. Torres (New York: Routledge, 2009), 61–83.
5 Christopher Campbell, Catherine Taylor, Elizabeth Meyer, Tracey Peter, Janice Ristock, and Donn Short, "Overcoming Barriers: Addressing Educators' Misconceptions and Fears about LGBTQ2+-Inclusive Education," *EdCan Network*. May 17, 2019). <www.edcan.ca> [perma.cc/T55Y-QKVN].
6 See Short, *Don't Be So Gay!* and *Am I Safe Here?* Introduction, note 4.
7 See Walton, Introduction, note 4.
8 Ibid.
9 Ibid.
10 Ibid.
11 Human Rights Commissions in some jurisdictions do have the power to undertake systemic investigations and to order systemic remedies, but these powers are rarely used.
12 See Dan Olweus, *Aggression in the Schools: Bullies and Whipping Boys* (Washington, DC: Hemisphere, 1978).
13 See Walton, Introduction, note 4.
14 See Short, *Am I Safe Here?* Introduction, note 4.
15 See Government of Saskatchewan, "Anti-Bullying." <www.education.gov.sk.ca/Anti-Bullying/Educators> [perma.cc/Q4PX-ESMP].
16 See Public Health Agency of Canada, "Questions and Answers: Sexual Orientation in Schools," *Public Health Agency of Canada*. <librarypdf.catie.ca/ATI-20000s/26288E.pdf> [perma.cc/Z28J-QTQX].
17 Ibid.
18 See Taylor et al., *The Every Teacher Project*, Chapter 1, note 50.
19 Ibid.

CHAPTER 3: VOICES THAT MATTER

1 *Hall (Litigation Guardian of) v Powers* (2002), 59 OR (3d) 423, 213 DLR (4th) 308 (Ont Sup Ct J) [*Hall*].

2. See *North Vancouver School District No 44 v Jubran*, 2005 BCCA 201 [*Jubran*], rev'g 2003 BCSC 6, [2003] WWR 288.
3. See *PT v Alberta*, 2018 ABQB 496 [*PT v Alberta*].
4. *Chamberlain v Surrey School District No 36*, 2002 SCC 86 [*Chamberlain*].
5. *TWU v BCCT*, Chapter 1, note 15.
6. *Kempling v British Columbia College of Teachers*, 2005 BCCA 327 [*Kempling*].
7. On the importance of the direct voice in such matters, see Bruce MacDougall, "The Direct Voice in Legal Discussions on Equality," *UBC Law Review* 44, 1 (2011): 181.
8. *Bill 10, An Act to Amend the Alberta Bill of Rights to Protect Our Children*, 3rd Sess, 28th Leg, Alberta, 63 Elizabeth II, 2014 [*Bill 10*].
9. *School Act*, RSA 2000, c S-3.
10. *Bill 24, An Act to Support Gay-Straight Alliances*, 3rd Sess, 29th Leg, Alberta, 2017 [*Bill 24*].
11. *PT v Alberta*, Chapter 3, note 3.
12. Ibid., para 35.
13. Ibid., para 18.
14. Ibid., para 18.
15. Ibid., para 38.
16. Ibid., para 37.
17. Ibid., para 41.
18. Ibid., paras 88–94.
19. *PT v Alberta* 2018 ABCA 312 [*PT ABCA*], 112.
20. Ibid., para 39.
21. Ibid., para 40.
22. *Bill 8, Education Amendment Act*, 1st Sess, 30th Leg, Alberta, 2019 (assented to 17 July, 2020), SA 2019, c 7. [*Bill 8*]. *Bill 8* amended Alberta's *Education Act* RSA, 2012 c E-0.3. The *Education Act* was passed in 2012, intended to replace the *School Act*, Chapter 3, note 9, which had governed education in Alberta for almost three decades. The *Education Act* was amended in 2015, and passed, but never proclaimed into law. When the NDP took office, they left the *School Act* in place, preferring to review the *Education Act*. The *Education Act*, as amended by *Bill 8*, came into force under the UCP government on September 1, 2019, repealing the *School Act*.
23. Caley Ramsay, "Controversial Alberta Education Bill Passes after Marathon Debate," *Global News*. July 5, 2019. <https://globalnews.ca/news/5463387/alberta-legislature-bill-8-education-gay-straight-alliances-debate/> perma.cc/Z9ME-CL5N].
24. For Manitoba, see *Bill 18*, Chapter 1, note 1. For Ontario, see *Bill 13*, Chapter 1, note 22.
25. Freedom of Information and Protection of Privacy Act, RSA 2000 c F-25 [*FOIP*]; see also Personal Information Protection Act, RSA 2003, c P-6.5 [*PIPA*].
26. *FOIP*, Chapter 3, note 25, s 40(1)(ee).
27. *FOIP*, Chapter 3, note 25, s 40(4).
28. Alanna Smith, "LGBTQ Youth Demand Meeting with Alberta Premier Jason Kenney," *Calgary Herald*. July 22, 2019. <https://calgaryherald.com/news/local-news/lgbtq-youth-demand-meeting-with-alberta-premier-jason-kenney> [perma.cc/W3YB-35U2].
29. Ibid.
30. Ibid.

31 For Ontario, see *Bill 13*, Chapter 1, note 22. For Manitoba, see *Bill 18*, Chapter 1, note 1. For Alberta, see *Bill 10*, Chapter 3, note 8.
32 See *Jubran v North Vancouver School District No 44*, 2002 BCHRT 10, 42 CHRR D/273, rev'd 2003 BCSC 6, [2003] WWR 288, aff'd *Jubran BCCA*, Chapter 3, note 2.
33 *Jubran BCCA*, Chapter 3, note 2, para 54.
34 Justice Gonthier was one of two dissenting voices in this judgment. Yet, the majority did not disagree with his analysis about the common law and *Charter* basis of parental rights.
35 See *Chamberlain*, Chapter 3, note 4, para 102.
36 Ibid., paras 106-8. According to section 7 of the *Charter*: "Everyone has the right to life, liberty, and security of the person and the right not to be deprived thereof except in accordance with the principles of fundamental justice."
37 *Chamberlain*, Chapter 3, note 4, para 106. See also *R v Jones*, [1986] 2 SCR 284 at 319-20. In *R v Jones*, Justice Wilson likewise articulated the view that s 7 includes the parental right to bring up and educate one's children in line with one's conscientious belief. While describing this right, she stated: "The relations of affection between an individual and his family and his assumption of duties and responsibilities towards them are central to the individual's sense of self and of his place in the world. The right to educate his children is one facet of this larger concept." This has been widely recognized. Article 8(1) of the *European Convention for the Protection of Human Rights and Fundamental Freedoms*, 213 U.N.T.S. 222 (1950), states, in part: "Everyone has the right to respect for his private and family life ..." Particularly relevant to the appellant's claim is Article 2 of Protocol No. 1 of the Convention: "No person shall be denied the right to education. In the exercise of any functions which it assumes in relation to education and to teaching, the State shall respect the right of parents to ensure such education and teaching in conformity with their own religious and philosophical convictions." Furthermore, see *International Covenant on Civil and Political Rights*, 19 December, 1966, 999 UNTS 181 art 18(4) (entered into force 23 March 1976, accession by Canada 19 May 1976) [*ICCPR*]. Article 18(4) of the *ICCPR*, reads as follows: "The States Parties to the present Covenant undertake to have respect for the liberty of parents ... to ensure the religious and moral education of their children in conformity with their own convictions." Finally, see *Universal Declaration of Human Rights*, GA Res 217A (III), UNGAOR, 3rd Sess, Supp No 13, UN Doc A/810 (1948) 7, s 26(3). That section states, "[p]arents have a prior right to choose the kind of education that shall be given to their children."
38 *Chamberlain*, Chapter 3, note 4, para 108.
39 Ibid., para 103. Neglect and abuse are obvious examples where state intervention is justified.
40 *Halton Children's Aid Society v GK*, 2015 ONCJ 307, 254 ACWS (3d) 862 [*Halton*].
41 Ibid.
42 Ibid., 95.
43 Ibid., 117.
44 Ibid., 89.
45 See *Serup v British Columbia School District No 57* (1987), 14 BCLR (2d). This is discussed and elaborated on in Terri Sussel, *Controversies in School Law: A Handbook for Educational Administrators* (Vancouver: EduServ, 1990), 89ff.

46 Sussel, ibid., 89: "Masturbation, Premarital Sex, Sex Games among Pre-pubescent Children, and Sex with Animals."
47 Ibid.
48 *PT v Alberta*, Chapter 3, note 3.
49 *Chamberlain*, Chapter 3, note 4.
50 Ibid., paras 33 and 65.
51 *SL v Commission*, Chapter 1, note 25.
52 Ibid., para 40.
53 *PT v Alberta*, Chapter 3, note 3, para 15.
54 *Chamberlain*, Chapter 3, note 4, para 214.
55 *Ross*, Chapter 1, note 27, para 46.
56 *Chamberlain*, Chapter 3, note 4, para 115.

CHAPTER 4: "WHAT'S NEW?"

1 See Bruce MacDougall, "The Celebration of Same-Sex Marriage," *Ottawa Law Review*, 32, 2 (2000): 235.
2 See Paul Clarke and Bruce MacDougall, "The Case for Gay-Straight Alliances (GSAs) in Canada's Public Schools: An Educational Perspective," *Education and Law Journal*, 21 (2000): 143 [Clarke and MacDougall, "Educational Perspective"]; See also *PT v Alberta*, Chapter 3, note 3.
3 See *LSBC v TWU*, Introduction, note 11, para 64.
4 See MacDougall and Short, Chapter 1, note 46.
5 *Hall*, Chapter 3, note 1.
6 *Ontario (Human Rights Commission) v Christian Horizons*, 2010 ONSC 2105, 102 OR (3d) 267.
7 *Chamberlain*, Chapter 3, note 4.
8 See Clarke and MacDougall, "Educational Perspective," Chapter 4, note 2. See also *PT v Alberta*, Chapter 3, note 3.
9 *Vriend*, Chapter 1, note 20.
10 For example, see the description of the litigants in the BC same-sex marriage case: *EGALE Canada Inc v Canada (Attorney General)*, 2001 BCSC 1365, paras 15–43, [2001] 11 WWR 685, rev'd 2003 BCCA 251. Justice Pitfield said of the couples at paras 44–45: "The profiles portray a uniform pattern: couples who are ordinary citizens in ordinary jobs and walks of life who share children, friends, family, property, companionship, self and community responsibility, affection and commitment. These traits are no different from the traits that are characteristic of marriages in our community. The difference between these and heterosexual couples is that the former choose and prefer a committed relationship and sexual relations with a person of the same, rather than opposite, sex."
11 *Reference re: Section 293 of the Criminal Code of Canada*, 2011 BCSC 1588.
12 See *Amselem*, Chapter 1, note 25.
13 *Nichols v MJ*, 2009 SKQB 299, para 10, [2009] 10 WWR 513.
14 *Hendricks v Québec (Procureur-Général)*, [2002] RJQ 2506, para 29.

15 Ibid.
16 *Chiang v Vancouver Board of Education*, 2009 BCHRT 319, 68 CHRR D/128 [*Chiang*].
17 Ibid.
18 See e.g., Sue-Ellen Jacobs, Wesley Thomas, and Sabine Lang, eds., *Two-Spirit People: Native American Gender Identity, Sexuality, and Spirituality* (Chicago: University of Illinois Press, 1997).
19 *B(R) v Children's Aid Society of Metropolitan Toronto*, [1995] 1 SCR 315 at 435.
20 See Shauna Van Praagh, "Religion, Custody and a Child's Identities," *Osgoode Hall Law Journal*, 35, 2 (1997): 309.
21 *Multani v Commission scolaire Marguerite-Bourgeoys*, 2006 SCC 6 [*Multani*].
22 *Amselem*, Chapter 1, note 25, 69.
23 See *Nixon v Vancouver Rape Relief Society*, 2002 BCHRT 1, rev'd 2003 BCSC 1936, rev'd 2005 BCCA 601, and leave to appeal to SCC refused [*Nixon*]. See also barbara findlay, "Real Women: Kimberly Nixon v Vancouver Rape Relief," *UBC Law Review*, 36, 1 (2003): 57.
24 See *Jubran BCCA*, Chapter 3, note 2.
25 Richard Moon, "Introduction: Law and Religious Pluralism in Canada," *Law and Religious Pluralism in Canada*, edited by Moon (Vancouver: UBC Press, 2008), 1–15.
26 Ibid.
27 For scholarship dealing with positive attitudes toward homosexuality in Biblical times, see John Boswell, *Christianity, Social Tolerance & Homosexuality* (Chicago: University of Chicago Press, 1980) who claimed that brotherhood unions between two men were an early form of same-sex marriage.
28 *Chamberlain*, Chapter 3, note 4, para 150.
29 Alfred Denning, *The Changing Law* (London: Stevens & Sons Ltd, 1953) at 99, 122, cited in Iain T. Benson, "Notes Towards a (Re)Definition of the Secular," *UBC Law Review*, 33, 3 (2000): 520 at 527.
30 See Andrew Sharpe, *Transgender Jurisprudence: Dysphoric Bodies of Law* (London: Cavendish Publications, 2002).
31 See *Nixon*, Chapter 4, note 23.
32 See Jena McGill and Kyle Kirkup, "Locating the Trans Subject in Canadian Law: XY v Ontario," *Windsor Review of Legal and Social Issues* 96, 33 (2013): 1; Elaine Craig, "Trans-Phobia and the Relational Production of Gender," *Hastings Women's Law Journal* 18, 2 (2007): 137.
33 See Dana Phillips, "The Prude in the Law: Why the Polygamy Reference Is All about Sex," *Appeal*, 19 (2014): 151.
34 See ibid., involving a student (wrongly) identified as gay. See also Bruce MacDougall, *Queer Judgments*, Chapter 1, note 32, 98; Gerald Unks, ed., *The Gay Teen: Educational Practice and Theory for Lesbian, Gay, and Bisexual Adolescents* (London: Routledge, 1995); Andi O'Conor, "Who Gets Called Queer in School? Lesbian, Gay and Bisexual Teenagers, Homophobia, and High School," *High School Journal*, 77, 2 (1994): 7.
35 *Chamberlain*, Chapter 3, note 4.
36 *Vriend*, Chapter 1, note 20, para 103.

37 *Hall*, Chapter 3, note 1, para 15.
38 *SL v Commission*, Chapter 1, note 25.
39 See ibid. See also *Zylberberg v Sudbury Board of Education (1988)*, 65 OR (2d) 641 (CA); *Canadian Civil Liberties Assn v Ontario (Minister of Education) (1990)*, 71 OR (2d) 341 (CA).
40 See *SL v Commission*, Chapter 1, note 25, para 32.
41 Ibid., para 40.
42 *Chamberlain*, Chapter 3, note 4, para 66.

CHAPTER 5: MAKING SPACES, MAKING COMMUNITY

1 Samantha Craggs, "Religious Hamilton Dad Not an 'Advocate for Ignorance,' He Says," *CBC*. September 12, 2012. <www.cbc.ca/> [perma.cc/LYT3-Q5VB].
2 *ET v Hamilton-Wentworth District School Board*, 2017 ONCA 893 [*ET v Hamilton-Wentworth*], para 2.
3 Ibid., para 13.
4 *ET v Hamilton-Wentworth*, Chapter 5, note 2.
5 *Education Act*, RSO 1990, c E.2, s 169.1(1).
6 See Alexandra Posadzki, "Vancouver School Board Revises Gender Identities Policy," *Globe and Mail*. June 17, 2014. <perma.cc/ZKL4-NFS7>.
7 See Wendy Stueck, "Archdiocese of Vancouver Agrees to Accommodate Transgender Students," *Globe and Mail*. July 16, 2014. <perma.cc/8B99-QCAK>.
8 *Hall*, Chapter 3, note 1.
9 Ibid., para 41.
10 Ibid., para 43.
11 *Chamberlain*, Chapter 3, note 4.
12 Ibid., para 21.
13 See *NS*, Introduction, note 11.
14 *ET v Hamilton-Wentworth*, Chapter 5, note 1.
15 See *PT v Alberta*, Chapter 3, note 3.
16 See *Buterman v Greater St. Albert Catholic Regional Division No 29*, 2014 AHRC 8 [*Buterman*].
17 See e.g., *School Act*, RSBC 1996, c 412, s 76(2). Section 76(2) states that teachers must "inculcate the highest moral standards."
18 *Attis v Board of Education of District 15 et al. (1993)*, 142 NBR (2d) 1–35 (CA).
19 *Kempling*, Chapter 3, note 6. Note that the Court of Appeal did not consider s 2(a) *Charter* arguments dealing with freedom of religion.
20 Ibid.
21 Ibid., para 79.
22 Ibid., para 73.
23 Ibid., para 79.
24 *Ross*, Chapter 1, note 27.
25 Ibid., para 70.
26 Ibid., para 91.

27 Ibid., para 44. The court's reference to the teacher as *medium* is borrowed from the work of Allison Reyes, who considers the importance of teachers in the education process and the impact that they bear upon the system. See Allison Reyes, "Freedom of Expression and Public School Teachers," *Dalhousie Journal of Legal Studies*, 4, 35 (1995): 42. As Reyes notes: "Teachers are a significant part of the unofficial curriculum because of their status as 'medium.' In a very significant way the transmission of prescribed 'messages' (values, beliefs, knowledge) depends on the fitness of the 'medium' (the teacher)."
28 *Ross*, Chapter 1, note 27, para 45.
29 See Jen Gerson, "Discrimination Case Pits Transgender Rights against Those of a Religious School after Teacher Fired for Changing Gender," *National Post*. May 11, 2014. <nationalpost.com/news/Canada> [perma.cc/HRY8-75QA]. See also *Buterman*, Chapter 5, note 16. A substitute teacher was removed from the school's substitute teacher's list because he informed the school that he was transgender and was going to undergo transitional surgery over the summer.
30 See *Chiang*, Chapter 4, note 16, and *Kempling*, Chapter 3, note 6.
31 *Caldwell v Stuart*, [1984] 2 SCR 603.
32 Ibid.
33 *Hall*, Chapter 3, note 1.
34 See *Chamberlain*, Chapter 3, note 4 (school context); *TWU v BCCT*, Chapter 1, note 15 (university context).
35 See "Edmonton School Board Drops Abstinence-Based Sex Ed after Complaint," *CBC*. July 11, 2014. <www.cbc.ca> [perma.cc/Q9VT-NJHH].
36 *ET v Hamilton-Wentworth*, Chapter 5, note 2, para 28 citing *SL v Commission*, Chapter 1, note 25.
37 *ET v Hamilton-Wentworth*, Chapter 5, note 2, para 37.

CONCLUSION: GETTING THERE

1 Jon Young, Benjamin Levin, and Dawn Wallin, *Understanding Canadian Schools: An Introduction to Educational Administration*, 4th ed. (Scarborough: Nelson, 2007).
2 Ibid., 228.
3 Michael Haralambos and Martin Holborn, *Sociology: Themes and Perspectives*, 3rd ed. (London: Collins Educational, 1991).
4 Ibid.
5 See Taylor et al., *The Every Teacher Project*, Chapter 1, note 50.
6 Ibid.
7 Ibid.
8 See Short, *Don't Be So Gay!* Introduction, note 4.
9 Ibid.
10 Catherine Taylor, Tracey Peter, Christopher Campbell, Elizabeth Meyer, Janice Ristock, and Donn Short, "Gaps between Beliefs, Perceptions and Practices: The Every Teacher Project on LGBTQ-Inclusive Education in Canadian Schools." In "Special Issue on International Perspectives on Homophobic and Transphobic Bullying in Schools," ed. Joe Kosciw and Oren Pizmony-Levy, *Journal of LGBT Youth* 13, 1–2 (2016): 112–40.

11 Ibid.
12 Ibid.
13 *The Education Act*, SS 1995, c E-0.2, 1995 at s 175(2)(a).
14 B.S. Bloom, "Innocence in Education," *School Review*, 80 (1972): 333.

Bibliography

PRIMARY SOURCES

Legislation: Canada

Bill 8, Education Amendment Act, 1st Sess, 30th Leg, Alberta, 2019 (assented to 17 July, 2020), SA 2019, c 7.

Bill 10, An Act to Amend the Alberta Bill of Rights to Protect Our Children, 3rd Sess, 28th Leg, Alberta, 2015 (assented to 19 March 2015), SA 2015, c 1.

Bill 13, An Act to Amend the Education Act with Respect to Bullying and Other Matters, 1st Sess, 40th Leg, Ontario (assented to 19 June 2012), SO 2012, c 5.

Bill 18, The Public Schools Amendment Act (Safe and Inclusive Schools), 2nd Sess, 40th Leg, Manitoba, 2013.

Bill 24, An Act to Support Gay Straight Alliances, 3rd Sess, 29th Leg, Alberta, 2017 (assented to 15 December 2017), SA 2017, c 30.

Canadian Charter of Rights and Freedoms, Part 1 of the *Constitution Act, 1982*, being Schedule B to the *Canada Act 1982* (UK), 1982, c 11.

Education Act, RSA 2012, c E-0.3.

Education Act, RSO 1990, c E 2.

Education Act, SS 1995, c E-0.2.

Freedom of Information and Protection of Privacy Act, RSA 2000 c F-2.

Human Rights Code, RSO 1990, c H 19.

Personal Information Protection Act, RSA 2003, c P-6.5.

Saskatchewan Human Rights Code, 2018, S 2018, c S-24.2.

School Act, RSA 2000, c S-3.

School Act, RSBC 1996, c 412.

Legislation: International

Convention on the Rights of the Child, GA Res 44/25, UNGAOR, 44th Sess, Supp No 49, UN Doc A/44/49 (1989) 166.

Council of Europe, ECHR, 1950, *Convention for the Protection of Human Rights and Fundamental Freedoms*, 213 UNTS 222 (1950).

International Covenant on Civil and Political Rights, 19 December 1966, 999 UNTS 181 (entered into force 23 March 1976, accession by Canada 19 May 1976).

Universal Declaration of Human Rights, GA Res 217A (III), UNGAOR, 3rd Sess, Supp No 13, UN Doc A/810 (1948) 7.

JURISPRUDENCE

Attis v Board of Education of District 15 et al. (1993), 142 NBR (2d) 1 (CA).
B (R) v Children's Aid Society of Metropolitan Toronto, [1995] 1 SCR 315.
Buterman v Greater St. Albert Catholic Regional Division No. 29, 2014 AHRC 8.
Caldwell v Stuart, [1984] 2 SCR 603.
Canadian Civil Liberties Assn v Ontario (Minister of Education) (1990), 71 OR (2d) 341 (CA).
Chamberlain v Surrey School District No 36, 2002 SCC 86.
Chiang v Vancouver Board of Education, 2009 BCHRT 319.
Dagenais v Canadian Broadcasting Corp., [1994] 3 SCR 835.
EGALE Canada Inc. v Canada (Attorney General), 2001 BCSC 1365, [2001] 11 WWR 685, rev'd 2003 BCCA 251.
Egan v Canada, [1995] 2 SCR 513.
ET v Hamilton-Wentworth District School Board, 2017 ONCA 893.
Hall (Litigation Guardian of) v Powers (2002), 59 OR (3d) 423, 213 DLR (4th) 308 (Ont Sup Ct J).
Halton Children's Aid Society v GK, 2015 ONCJ 307.
Hendricks v Québec (Procureur-Général), [2002] RJQ 2506.
Jubran v North Vancouver School District No 44, 2002 BCHRT 10.
Kempling v British Columbia College of Teachers, 2005 BCCA 327.
Law Society of British Columbia v Trinity Western University, 2018 SCC 32.
Loyola High School v Quebec (Attorney General), 2015 SCC 12.
Multani v Commission scolaire Marguerite-Bourgeoys, 2006 SCC 6.
Nichols v MJ, 2009 SKQB 299.
Nixon v Vancouver Rape Relief Society, 2002 BCHRT 1, rev'd 2003 BCSC 1936, rev'd 2005 BCCA 601.
North Vancouver School District No. 44 v Jubran, 2005 BCCA 201, rev'g 2003 BCSC 6.
Ontario (Human Rights Commission) v Christian Horizons, 2010 ONSC 2105.
PT v Alberta, 2018 ABQB 496.
PT v Alberta, 2018 ABCA 312.
R v Big M Drug Mart, [1985] 1 SCR 295.
R v Crawford, [1995] 1 SCR 858.
R v Jones, [1986] 2 SCR 284.
R v Mentuck, 2001 SCC 76.
R v NS, 2012 SCC 72.
Reference re Same-Sex Marriage, 2004 SCC 79.
Reference re: Section 293 of the Criminal Code of Canada, 2011 BCSC 1588.
Ross v New Brunswick School District No. 15, [1996] 1 SCR 825.
Saskatchewan (Human Rights Commission) v Whatcott, 2013 SCC 11.

Serup v British Columbia School District No 57 (1987), 14 BCLR (2d).
SL v Commission scolaire des Chênes, 2012 SCC 7.
Syndicat Northcrest v Amselem, 2004 SCC 47.
Trinity Western University v British Columbia College of Teachers, 2001 SCC 31.
Trinity Western University v Law Society of Upper Canada, 2018 SCC 33.
Vriend v Alberta, [1998] 1 SCR 493.
Zylberberg v Sudbury Board of Education (1988), 65 OR (2d) 641 (CA).

SECONDARY SOURCES

Abramovich, Alex. "No Fixed Address: Young, Queer, and Restless." In *Youth Homelessness in Canada: Implications for Policy and Practice*, edited by Stephen Gaetz, Bill O'Grady, et al. Toronto: Canadian Observatory on Homelessness, 2017.

Batlinski, Thadeus, "Manitoba Anti-bullying Bill 18 May Force Gay-Straight Alliance Clubs on Independent Religious School." *LifeSite*, March 1, 2013. <www.lifesitenews.com> [perma.cc/89CH-UAPD].

"Bella's Family Reaches Transgender-Rights Settlement with School Division." *Winnipeg Sun*, March 11, 2016. <https://winnipegsun.com/2016/03/11/bellas-family-reaches-transgender-rights-settlement-with-school-division> [perma.cc/M596-WCQF].

Bloom, BS. "Innocence in Education." *School Review*, 80, no. 3 (May 1972): 333.

Boswell, Jon. *Christianity, Social Tolerance & Homosexuality*. Chicago: University of Chicago Press, 1980.

Burr, Grant. "Wiens wins $70,000 scholarship." *The Carillon*, May 29, 2014. <www.winnigpegfreepress.com/thecarillon> [perma.cc/ZR88-JLE3].

Callaghan, Tonya. *That's So Gay: Homosexuality in Canadian Catholic Schools*. Saarbrucken: AV Akademikerverlag, 2012.

–. *Heterosexism and Transphobia in Canadian Catholic Schools*. Toronto: University of Toronto Press, 2018.

Campbell, Christopher, Catherine Taylor, Elizabeth Meyer, Tracey Peter, Janice Ristock, and Donn Short. "Overcoming Barriers: Addressing Educators' Misconceptions and Fears about LGBTQ2+-Inclusive Education." *EdCan Network*. May 17, 2019. <www.edcan.ca> [perma.cc/T55Y-QKVN].

Canadian Press. "Human rights complaint prompts new gender policy in Vancouver Catholic Schools." *CBC Canada*, July 16, 2014. <www.cbc.ca/> [perma.cc/MK63-3F6K].

Clarke, Paul and Bruce MacDougall. "The Case for Gay-Straight Alliances (GSAs) in Canada's Public Schools: An Educational Perspective." *Education Law Journal* 21 (2000): 143.

Cloutier, Danelle. "Transgender girl's human rights complaint against school division in Winnipeg resolved." *CBC*, March 11, 2016. <www.cbc.ca/news> [perma.cc/PF9W-DH8Q].

Coutts, Matthew. "Manitoba Christian School Opposes Anti-bullying Law Protecting Homosexual Clubs." *Daily Brew*, February 26, 2013. <ca.news.yahoo.com> [perma.cc/49Q3-KP7Y].

Craig, Elaine. "Trans-Phobia and the Relational Production of Gender." *Hastings Women's Law Journal* 18, no. 2 (2007): 137.

Craggs, Samantha. "Religious Hamilton Dad Not an 'Advocate for Ignorance,' He Says." he says." *CBC News*, September 12, 2012. <www.cbc.ca> [perma.cc/8S9X-95B6].

Crenshaw, KW. "Mapping the Margins: Intersectionality, Identity Politics, and Violence against Women of Color." *Stanford Law Review* 43, no. 6 (1991): 1241.

Denning, Alfred. *The Changing Law*. London: Stevens and Sons, 1953, at 99, 122. Cited in Benson, Iain T. "Notes Towards a (Re)Definition of the Secular." *UBC Law Review* 33, no. 3 (2000): 520.

"Edmonton School Board Drops Abstinence-Based Sex Ed after Complaint." *CBC News*, July 11, 2014. <www.cbc.ca> [perma.cc/Q9VT-NJHH].

findlay, barbara. "Real Women: Kimberly Nixon v Vancouver Rape Relief." *UBC Law Review* 36, no. 1 (2003): 57.

Gerson, Jen. "Discrimination Case Pits Transgender Rights against Those of a Religious School after Teacher Fired for Changing Gender." *National Post*, May 11, 2014. <nationalpost.com/news/Canada> [perma.cc/HRY8-75QA].

Government of Saskatchewan. "Anti-Bullying." <www.education.gov.sk.ca/Anti-Bullying/Educators> [perma.cc/Q4PX-ESMP].

"GSA Told Not to Advertise: Student. School Board Accused of Discrimination." *Winnipeg Free Press*, March 1, 2013. <www.winnipegfreepress.com> [perma.cc/XE74-KQ3P].

Haralambos, Michael, and Martin Holborn. *Sociology: Themes and Perspectives*, 3rd ed. London: Collins Educational, 1991.

Jacobs, Sue-Ellen, Wesley Thomas, and Sabine Lang, eds. *Two-Spirit People: Native American Gender Identity, Sexuality, and Spirituality*. Chicago: University of Illinois Press, 1997.

Kaschor, Kim. "Diversity Policy Needs Update, Says Manitoba LGBTQ Advocate Evan Wiens." *CBC News*, April 25, 2016. <www.cbc.ca> [perma.cc/2RMT-YBYD].

MacDougall, Bruce. "The Celebration of Same-Sex Marriage." *Ottawa Law Review* 32, no. 2 (2000): 235.

–. "The Direct Voice in Legal Discussions on Equality." *UBC Law Review* 44, no. 1 (2011): 181.

–. *Queer Judgments: Homosexuality, Expression and the Courts in Canada*. Toronto: University of Toronto Press, 2000.

MacDougall, Bruce, and Donn Short. "Religion-Based Claims for Impinging on Queer Citizenship." *Dalhousie Law Journal* 33, no. 2 (2010): 133.

"Manitoba Human Rights Commission to Hear Transgender Girl's Case in July." *CBC*, January 12, 2016. <https://www.cbc.ca/news/canada/manitoba/manitoba-human-rights-commission-to-hear-transgender-girl-s-case> [perma.cc/5JVV-5PUG].

Martin, Nick. "Steinbach Bill 18." *Winnipeg Free Press*, March 7, 2013. <www.winnipegfreepress.com> [perma.cc/49Q3-KP7Y].

McConnell, Elizabeth A., Michelle Birkett, and Brian Mustanski. "Families Matter: Social Support and Mental Health Trajectories among Lesbian, Gay, Bisexual and Transgender Youth." *Journal of Adolescent Health* 59, no. 6 (2016): 674.

McGill, Jena, and Kyle Kirkup. "Locating the Trans Subject in Canadian Law: XY v Ontario." *Windsor Review of Legal and Social Issues* 33, no. 1 (2013): 96.

McLaren, Peter. "Critical Pedagogy: A Look at the Major Concepts." In *The Critical Pedagogy Reader*, 2nd ed., edited by Antonia Darder, Marta P. Baltodano, and Rodolfo D. Torres, 61. New York: Routledge, 2009.

Moon, Richard. "Introduction: Law and Religious Pluralism in Canada." In *Law and Religious Pluralism in Canada*, edited by Moon, 1. Vancouver: UBC Press.

Myer, Elizabeth, Tracey Peter, Janice Ristock, and Catherine Taylor. "Conflicting Beliefs, Perceptions and Behaviors." In "Special Issue on International Perspectives on Homophobic and Transphobic Bullying in Schools," ed. Joe Kosciw and Oren Pizmony-Levy, *Journal of LGBT Youth* 13, nos. 1–2 (2016): 112–40.

Nienow, Flavio. "Schools in Rural Areas Lack Support for LGBTQ Students." *Shellbrook Chronicle*, May 23, 2014. <shellbrookchronicle.com> [perma.cc/DDY6-867C].

O'Conor, Andi. "Who Gets Called Queer in School? Lesbian, Gay and Bisexual Teenagers, Homophobia, and High School." *High School Journal* 77, no. 2 (1994): 7.

Olweus, Dan. *Aggression in the Schools: Bullies and Whipping Boys*. Washington, DC: Hemisphere, 1978.

Ontario Catholic Schools Trustees' Association. "'Respecting Difference': A Resource for Catholic Schools in the Province of Ontario." *Diocese of London*, January 25, 2012. <dol.ca> [perma.cc/5RQB-BV36].

Phillips, Dana. "The Prude in the Law: Why the Polygamy Reference Is All about Sex." *Appeal* 19 (2014): 151.

Posadzki, Alexandra. "Vancouver School Board Revises Gender Identities Policy." *Globe and Mail*, June 17, 2014. <www.theglobeandmail.com> [perma.cc/ZKL4-NFS7].

Public Health Agency of Canada. "Questions and Answers: Sexual Orientation in Schools." <librarypdf.catie.ca> [perma.cc/Z28J-QTQX].

Ramsay, Caley. "Controversial Alberta Education Bill Passes after Marathon Debate." *Global News*, July 5, 2019. <https://globalnews.ca/news/5463387/alberta-legislature-bill-8-education-gay-straight-alliances-debate/> perma.cc/Z9ME-CL5N].

Regina Board of Education SD No 4. "Regina Public Schools Board Policy 1 – Division Foundational Statements." Last modified May 28, 2019. <www.reginapublicschools.ca/board_policies> [perma.cc/YH8H-7TTU].

Reyes, Allison. "Freedom of Expression and Public School Teachers." *Dalhousie Journal of Legal Studies* 4 (1995): 35.

Russell, Stephen T., Joseph Kosciw, Stacey Horn & Elizabeth Saewyc. "Social Policy Report: Safe Schools Policy for 2SLGBTQ+ Students." *Sharing Child and Youth Development Knowledge* (2010) 24, 4: 1 at 5.

Russell, Stephen T., and Stacey S. Horn. *Sexual Orientation, Gender Identity, and Schooling: The Nexus of Research, Practice, and Policy*. Oxford: Oxford University Press, 2017.

Seper, Franjo. "Persona Humana: Declaration on Certain Questions Concerning Sexual Ethics." *Vatican*, December 29, 1975. <www.vatican.va> [perma.cc/KUN3-EVQF].

"Sexual Orientation – Principles." *The Evangelical Fellowship of Canada*. Last accessed July 12, 2019. <bbnc.evangelicalfellowship.ca> [perma.cc/P3NC-AKGT].

Sharpe, Andrew. *Transgender Jurisprudence: Dysphoric Bodies of Law*. London: Cavendish Publications, 2002.

Short, Donn. *Am I Safe Here? LGBTQ Teens and Bullying*. Vancouver: On Point Press, 2017.

–. "Bound for Glory: Bill 18, The Public Schools Amendment Act (Safe and Inclusive Schools)." *Manitoba Law Journal* 36, no. 2 (2013): 115.
–. *Don't Be So Gay: Queers, Bullying and Making Schools Safe*. Vancouver: UBC Press, 2013.
–. "Queering Schools, GSAs and the Law." In *The Gay Agenda: Claiming Space, Identity & Justice*, edited by Gerald Walton, 327–43. New York: Peter Lang, 2014.
–. "Safe Schools: The Threat from Within?" *Education Canada* 51, no. 3 (2011): 4.
Smith, Alanna. "LGBTQ youth demand meeting with Alberta Premier Jason Kenney." *Calgary Herald*, July 22, 2019. <https://calgaryherald.com/news/local-news/lgbtq-youth-demand-meeting-with-alberta-premier-jason-kenney> [perma.cc/W3YB-35U2].
Stueck, Wendy. "Archdiocese of Vancouver agrees to accommodate transgender students." *Globe and Mail*, July 16, 2014. <www.theglobeandmail.com> [perma.cc/8B99-QCAK].
Sussel, Terri. *Controversies in School Law: A Handbook for Educational Administrators*. Vancouver: EduServ, 1990.
–. "Masturbation, Premarital Sex, Sex Games among Pre-pubescent Children, and Sex with Animals." Vancouver: EduServ, 1990.
Taylor, Catherine, Tracey Peter, Christopher Campbell, Elizabeth Meyer, Janice Ristock, and Donn Short. *The Every Teacher Project on LGBTQ-Inclusive Education in Canada's K-12 Schools*. Winnipeg: Manitoba Teachers' Society, 2015.
–. "Gaps between Beliefs, Perceptions and Practices: The Every Teacher Project on LGBTQ-Inclusive Education in Canadian Schools." In "Special Issue on International Perspectives on Homophobic and Transphobic Bullying in Schools," ed. Joe Kosciw and Oren Pizmony-Levy, *Journal of LGBT Youth* 13, nos. 1–2 (2016): 112–40.
Unks, Gerald, ed. *The Gay Teen: Educational Practice and Theory for Lesbian, Gay, and Bisexual Adolescents*. London: Routledge, 1995.
Van Praagh, Shauna. "Religion, Custody and a Child's Identities." *Osgoode Hall Law Journal* 35, no. 2 (1997): 309.
Walton, Gerald. "Bullying and Homophobia in Canadian Schools: The Politics of Policies, Programs and Educational Leadership." *Journal of Gay and Lesbian Issues in Education* 1, no. 4 (2003): 23.
–. "Bullying Widespread: A Critical Analysis of Research and Public Discourse on Bullying." *Journal of School Violence* 4, no. 1 (2005): 91.
–. "The Notion of Bullying through the Lens of Foucault and Critical Theory." *Journal of Educational Thought* 39, no. 1 (2005): 55.
Wingrove, Josh. "Gay teen holds the line for Manitoba bullying bill." *Globe and Mail*, March 17, 2013. <www.theglobeandmail.com> [perma.cc/R48B-N5DL].
Young, Jon, Benjamin Levin, and Dawn Wallin. *Understanding Canadian Schools: An Introduction to Educational Administration*, 4th ed. Scarborough: Nelson, 2007.
Zongrone, A.D., N.L. Truong, and J.G. Kosciw. *Erasure and Resilience: The Experiences of LGBTQ Students of Color, Native and Indigenous LGBTQ Youth in U.S. Schools*. New York: GLSEN, 2020.

Index

Note: page numbers in **bold** indicate definitions and case studies.

2SLGBTQ+ students: bullying and harassment of, 20, 46–47; burden of responsibility on, 74; coming out, 3–4; consideration of within legal processes, 64–67; legal constraints on, 19; outsider groups and, 124; rights of, 56; statistics about, 72

Abdalla Idris Ali, 91
absolute rights, 24–25, **25**, 30, **32**
abstinence, 124
access to school spaces, 104–5, 123–24. *See also* inclusion; schools
accommodations in schools, 16, 20, 38–39, 110–14, 122–23
activism, student-led, 20
administrators, 45–48, 56, 58, 61, 114, 130, 131
adults, 4, 66–67, 109–10, 114–21. *See also* administrators; parents; teachers
Alberta, 13, 26, 68–71, 73–74, 79, 123–24, 130
Alberta Bill of Rights, 69
Alberta Court of Appeal, 69, 71
Alberta human rights statute, 26
Allen, Nancy, 98
allies, 40, 44, 74–75

Amselem, Moïse, 28–29
anti-harassment policies. *See* bullying
anti-Semitism, 117
assault and harassment at school. *See* bullying
assemblies, school, 110–11
Attis v Board of Education of District 15 et al, 115
authenticity, 4, 21–22
A.Y. Jackson High School, 42

beliefs, right to act on *vs.* hold, 23–24, **24**
Bible, New Testament, 96
Bill 8, Alberta, 73–74
Bill 10, Alberta, 68
Bill 13, Ontario, 27, 37, 60
Bill 18, Manitoba, 20–24, 27, 34. *See also* bullying
Bill 24, Alberta, 68–69, 71, 73
binaries, of gender and sexuality, 85, 92–93, 97
birth control, 124
black-and-white thinking, 92
Black students, 51–52
Boys and Sex (book), 78
British Columbia, 14, 35–36, 48–49, 66, 78, 95, 109, 115

British Columbia College of Teachers (BCCT), 66, 115
British Columbia Supreme Court, 49
bullying: by adults, 4–5, 18; *Bill 18,* 20; broad conceptions of, 55, 57; changing views of, 59; cultural context of, 53, 58; cyberbullying, 42; definition, **48,** 49; experienced by Azmi Jubran, 48–49; homophobic and transphobic, 53; leading to suicide, 42; prevention of, 47; research on, 60; school policies preventing, 6, 14, 46, 47–48, 59. *See also* safety in school
Burgos, Dale, 4
Burgos, Elizabeth, 4, 18
Burgos, Isabella, 3–5
Burgos family, 17–18

Caldwell et al. v. Stuart et al. 1984 2 SCR 603, 122
Canadian Charter of Rights and Freedoms: competing rights claims and, 11, 24, 28; reading in sexual orientation, 27; section 1, 116, 117, 119; section 2(1), 94; section 2(a), 30, 69, 76, 94–95; section 2(b), 116, 117–18; section 7, 69, 76; section 15, 12, 22–23, 88, 117; on sexual orientation, 26–27, 62, 133
categorization, 89–90
Catholic Independent Schools of the Vancouver Archdiocese, 38
Catholic schools, 37. *See also* religious schools
celebration, 6, 101, 128, 131, 132. *See also* inclusion
Centre of Islamic Education in North America, 91
Chamberlain, James, 66
Chamberlain v Surrey School District No 36 2002 SCC 86, 76–77, **77,** 79, 81–82, 96, 101
characterization in courts, 95, 96
Chiang, Po Yu Emmy, 91
Chiang v Vancouver Board of Education, 91

children: "best interests of," 76–77; inclusion in legal processes, 64–68; rights of, 70, 75, 93–94; voices of, 97
Christian Fellowship Club, 91
Christianity, 11, 32–33, 91, 96, 106, 110
Christian Truth Activists, 32, **33**
clubs, school, 21, 113–14
cognitive dissonance, 80, 100
coming out, 3–4, 58, 74
competing rights scenarios: definition and background, **10,** 10–11, 27–28; GSAs as, 13–14; increases in, 133; of parents, 112–13; raised by Christopher Kempling, 66–67, 115–17; at school dances, 111; Trinity Western University, 14–15, 36
Conservative Party government of Alberta, 68, 73
Constitution Act, 1867, 111
cultural hierarchies, 56
cultural recognition, 16
culture, transforming school: fear of, 10, 47; GSAs' role in, 22; importance of for school safety, 6–7, 45–46, 58, 60, 134; principal's views on, 50–51; support from law, 11, 16, 61; through teacher training, 56
curriculum: changes in, 55, 56, 103, 105–7, 131–32, 134; definition, 126; hidden, **127,** 127–28, 131–32; official, **126,** 128, 132–33; third, 129–33
custody disputes, 63, 78
cyberbullying, 42, 55

dances, 111
Denning, Lord Alfred Thompson, 96
denominational schools. *See* religious schools
Deschamps, Justice Marie, 80
different realities, 101
discrimination: by Christopher Kempling, 66, 115–17; experienced by Azmi Jubran, 48–49; experienced by Gabriel Picard, 45; fear of, 98–99; prevention of in schools, 7; protection from, 13,

23, 26–27; in religious schools, 35–37; right to be free from, 7, 10, 89; training to prevent, 18, 55–56, 121

diversity: promotion of, 36, 80, 113, 125, 128, 130; of religious views, 81–82, 99, 125

dress policies in schools, 51–52, 109

Duerksen, Pastor, 21

Edmonton, Alberta, 123–24

Edmonton Pregnancy Care Centre, 123–24

education, right to, 23

Education Act (Ontario), 62

Education Act (Saskatchewan), 130

education and awareness, 7, 17, 37, 46, 50

education systems, 63

Egan v Canada, 23

equality, formal *vs.* substantive, **87**, 88

equality rights claims, 15, 26–28, 31, 66, 88, 111, 115

equity: culture of, 37, 129, 130; offices, 56; policies, 51; promoted in *Bill 18*, 34–35. *See also* inclusion

essentialism, 88–90, **89**, 92–93, 98

Ethics and Religious Culture (ERC) program, 99

Evangelical Foundation of Canada, 39

Evangelical Free Church of Canada, 66

evidence-based approaches to school change, 72

exclusion from school communities, 98–99, 104, 121–22, 124

faith-based schools. *See* religious schools

false teachings, 102

families and home environments: Burgos family, 17–18; hostility in, 42, 57, 78; religion in, 79, 100–1; stress from, 3; support from, 4–5, 46

Feenstra, Rev. George, 44

findlay, barbara, 39

First National Climate Survey on Homophobia, Biphobia and Transphobia in Canadian Schools, 60

fluidity, gender and sexual identity, 75, 86, 88, 92–93, 97–101

formal equality, **87**, 88

freedom of expression, 32, 35, 66, 115–18

freedom of religion, 6, 16, 22–25; *Bill 24*, Alberta and, 69; respect of, 47; scenarios of, 28–31; shaped by *R v Big M Drug Mart Ltd*, **32**; of students in school, 93–94

gay-straight alliances (GSAs): advocacy for, 60; benefits of attending for students, 9, 71–72, 131; founding by Evan Wiens, 22, 43; in Lakehead District School Board, 46; legal support for, 13–15, 20, 37, 130; parent attitudes toward, 76, 79, 81; participation in, 68, 114; requirement of in Alberta, 68–71; resistance to, 32, 42–43; rights infringement and, 31; school initiation of, 73–75, 103; as voluntary organizations, 80

gender identity, 3–5, 107–9. *See also* fluidity, gender and sexual identity; transgender identities

gender-sexuality alliances (GSAs). *See* gay-straight alliances (GSAs)

Globe and Mail, 21–22

Greek Orthodox Church, 102

Hall, Marc, 62–63, 65, 99, 111, 122

Halton Children's Aid Society v G.K., 78

Hamilton-Wentworth District School Board, 102

Handsworth Secondary School, 48

harassment and assault at school: of 2SLGBTQ+ allies, 74–75; old perspectives on, 42; prevalence of, 9, 72, 128–29; prevention of, 45–46, 130; research on, 60–61; right to be free of, 34. *See also* bullying

hate and hate speech, 32, **33**, 34, **34**, 119

heteronormativity: definition, 11, **12**; as a preconception, 84–85; in school cultures, 53, 94, 97, 130, 133; in school curriculum, 106
heterosexism, 14
hierarchies, cultural, 56, 107, 129, 133
hierarchy of rights, 25
high school prom, 62
holding *vs.* acting on beliefs, 120–21
homophobia: by Bill Whatcott, **33**; by Christopher Kempling, 66, 115–16, **116**; in comments and conversation, 72; definition, 8; as denouncing GSAs, 32; driven-bullying in schools, 53; education about, 124; experienced by Azmi Jubran, 48–49, **49**; experienced by Gabriel Picard, 45–46, **46**; experienced by Marc Hall, 62; hate speech and, 34; religious schools and, 39–40, 42; thriving in schools, 42, 128–29; through inaction, 132
homosexuality in the Bible, 96
Hubley, Jamie, 42
human rights: accommodation and access as, 108, 109; complaints, 5, 18, 32, 38–39, 45, 48–49, 91; defence of, 14, 24, 33–35; enforcement, 58; equality and, 88, 98; laws, 5, 13, 23, 26, 41, 89. *See also* Bill 18, Manitoba
Human Rights Code, 5, 13, 23, 45, **46**, 49
Human Rights Commission of Ontario, 46
Human Rights Tribunal in British Columbia, 48, 49

identities. *See* fluidity, gender and sexual identity; transgender identities
inclusion: of 2SLGBTQ+ students in schools, 16; associated with school safety, 51, 53, 129–32; awareness raising and, 37; celebration and, 6, 9, 36, 41, 51, 56–57, 101; of children and youth in legal processes, 64–68; generic approaches to, 21; impeded by preconceptions, 85–86; Isabella Burgos's experiences with, 4–5; in law school mandates, 35–36; obligation of schools to, 101; policies for, 41–42; promoted by Rev. George Feenstra, 44; recognition by law, 98, 99, 125; in school culture, 7, 55, 120–21; through school space use, 103–5
Indigenous peoples, 106
Indigenous students, 7, 8, 9
individuals, role of in change, 7
injunctions, 62, 69, 71, 72
inquiry and questioning, 86, 98
insiders, 104–5. *See also* exclusion from school communities; inclusion; outsiders
intersectionality, 7–8, **8**, 9, 128
invisibility, 42, 50
Irwin, Janis, 74
Islamic beliefs, 81

Jubran, Azmi, 48–50, 65, 75, 95, 134

Kempling, Christopher, 66, 115–17
Kempling v British Columbia College of Teachers 2004 BCSC 133, **116**
Kubik, Justice Johnna C., 70, 71, 72, 80

labels, 51–52
Lakehead District School Board, 45–46
language, legal, 65
Lauson, Doug, 39
law: essentialist approaches to, 89–90; human rights, 5, 13, 23, 26, 41, 89; new conservations in, 84–86; as policy statements, 41; privacy laws, 73–74; in support of 2SLGBTQ+ students, 7. *See also* individual *Bills*
law schools, 35–36
Law Society of British Columbia, 36
LeBel, Justice Louis, 81
legal complaints: children and youth voices in, 64–66; Dr. Steve Tourloukis, 102; fluidity in, 97–101; Gabriel Picard, 45–47; Marc Hall, 62

legal protection: of GSAs, 13–14, 69; lagging cultural recognition, 16; in modern contexts, 111; origins of, 12
legal structures, 12, 64–68, 88
legislators, views of, 98
liberty rights, 70–71
libraries, school, 112
listening to children and youth, 64–68

MacKinnon, Justice Danalyn, 99, 111
Manitoba: *Bill 18*, 22, 27, 35, 37, 68; Evan Wiens in, 20, 43; Isabella Burgos in, 4; legal allies in, 98; rights of GSAs in, 13, 60, 68, 73, 74, 130; *Schools Act* in, **48**
marginalization, 42, 46–47, 70, 97, 106, 127–28, 130
McLachlin, Chief Justice Beverley, 79–80, 101
McLaren, Peter, 54
mediator roles in courts, 63
Mennonite communities, 20
minority rights, 100
modern context, 111
Monsignor John Pereyma Catholic Secondary School, 62
Moon, Richard, 95
morality of sexuality, 96–97
Multani v Commission Scolaire Marguerite-Bourgeoys, 93
Muslims, 81–82, 91

name changes, 108–9
NDP government of Alberta, 68, 73, 74
NDP government of Manitoba, 20
New Brunswick, 115
Nigeria, 85
Nixon, Kimberly, 95, 96
normalization in law, 90, 93
norms and taboos, 84–86
North Vancouver, British Columbia, 48, 49
North Vancouver School District No 44 v Jubran 2005 BCCA 201, **49**
Notley, Rachel, 68

Ontario: *Bill 13* protests in, 27; *Bill 13* support in, 38; Court of Appeal in, 113, 125; GSA debates in, 15, 45–46; *Human Rights Code* in, 13; Marc Hall in, 62; obligation to provide inclusive schools, 103; *Respecting Difference* report, 37; rights of GSAs in, 42–43, 60, 68, 73, 74, 98, 124–25, 130; T.E.A.C.H. program in, 124
Ontario Catholic School Trustees' Association, 37
Ontario Court of Appeal, 113, 125
Ontario English Catholic Teachers Association (OECTA), 15, 38
oppression, 7, 54, 55, 124
othering, 51–52
outsiders, 104–5, 123–24

parents: control of education, 69, 76–80, 99–100, 112–13; diverse voices of, 80–83; notification of, 69–70, 73–74, 114
pedagogy, critical, 54
Picard, Ellen Chambers, 46
Picard, Gabriel, 45–46, **46,** 134; discussions with principal, 50–51
policies, school: anti-oppressive, 59–61; challenges in improving, 40; for school safety, 7, 51–54
polygamy, 90
Powers, Mr., 62
power shifts, 10
preconceptions, influence of on legislation, 16, 84–86, 92–96
pride parades, 43
Prince George, British Columbia, 78
principals, 4–5, 21–22, 47, 50–51, 69, 73, 130–31, 134
privacy laws, 73–74
privilege of heterosexuality, 55, 107, 129, 131
prom, high school, 62, 111
pronouns, 108, 109
public education, non-discrimination values of, 23, 116, **116,** 119

public funding for education, 35, 40
public good, 71

Quebec, 80, 91, 93, 95, 99, 100
Quebec Court of Appeal, 91
queerphobia, **8**, 42. *See also* homophobia; transphobia
Quesnel Cariboo Observer, 66
Quesnel School District, 66, 115
questions, 45–47

racist speech, 119
Regina Public Schools, 41
religion, definitions, 94–96
religious beliefs: in competing rights claims, 70, 125; definitions through cases, 28–29; exposure to at school, 80; expression of, 15, 115–16; influences on sexuality views, 78, 84–86, 91; intersections with sexuality, 92, 102–3; validity of, 30
religious freedom: of parents, 99–100, 102–3; perceived infringement of, 9–10, 13–15, 21, 27, 60, 62–63, 80; preconceptions of, 86–87; questions informing, 15–16
religious neutrality, 100
religious rights: definitions, 94–96; legal protection of, 13; as road block for inclusive schools, 6–7, 10
religious schools: 2SLGBTQ+ inclusion in, 35–37; Catholic schools in Ontario, 37–38; diverse views in, 122–23; Steinbach Christian High School, 21; teacher disqualification in, 120–22; Trinity Western University, 14; views on homosexuality of, 39–40
resistance, to GSAs, 6–7, 9–11, 14, 42, 54, 60, 68
Respecting Difference document, 37–38
responsibility, burden of, 74–76
rights: 2SLGBTQ+, 56; of children, 70, 75, 93; competing definition, **10**; to education, 23; hierarchy of, 25; of parents, 69–70, 76–80; questions of, 15–16
rights infringement: in competing rights scenarios, 27–30; need for evidence in religious claims, **99**, 113, 116, 125; new perspectives on, 31–35; perceptions of, 7, 22, 24, 133
risks and rewards, 4
River East Transcona School Division (RETSD), 3–5, 17–18
role models, teachers as, 115, 119, 131
Roman Catholic school boards. *See* religious schools
Ross, Malcolm, 117
Ross v New Brunswick School District No 15 1996 1 SCR 825, **81,** 117–19, **118**
rural areas, 37, 53
Russia, 85
R v Big M Drug Mart Ltd 1985 1 SCR 295, **32**

safety in school: for 2SLGBTQ+ students, 6–7, 27; adults and, 109–10; avenues toward, 129–32; changing perceptions of, 50–52, 130; definitions, 6; feeling unsafe at school, 9; freedom from discrimination, 115–17; Gabriel Picard questioning, 45–46, 50; hate speech and, 34; ignoring, 52–54; new conceptions of, 54–56; obligation to provide, 48–50; progress in, 56–58; protecting, 32; statistics for 2SLGBTQ+ students, 72
same-sex marriage, 28, 86, 87, 90, 91, 133
Saskatchewan, 23, 32–35, 37, 41, 59, 130
Saskatchewan Human Rights Code, 2018, 23
Saskatchewan Human Rights Commission, 32
Saskatchewan Human Rights Commission v Whatcott 2013 SCC11, **35**
Saskatchewan Human Rights Tribunal, 33
Saskatoon Public School Board, **33**

School Act, Alberta, 68, 71
school culture: cultivating inclusive, 55; impacts of negative, 72–73; perspectives on, 54; role of in anti-bullying policies, 59–60; toxic, 52
schools: access to spaces in, 104–5; activities, 107; assemblies, 110–11; boards, 41, 46; climate of, 128–29; clubs, 21; curriculum as spaces, 105–7; dances, 111; governance, 23; legal requirements of, 12; libraries, 112; offering diverse perspectives, 79–80, **81**, 99–101, 112, 125; outsiders and, 123–24; reform, 55–56; spaces, 103–4. *See also* principals; safety in school; teachers
schools, religious. *See* religious schools
secularism, 81
security, as school safety, 51–52, 129
security guards, 51, 52
segregation, 4–5
self-perceptions, 3–4, 91, 92
settlement agreements, 17–18, 45–47
sexuality and sexual orientation: bullying and, 5, 45; children and, 94; claims, 87–88; definitions, 96–97, 136n13; educational curriculum, 123–24; equality rights, 26–27; intersections with religious beliefs, 92; and religion, 11, 102–3
Short, Donn, 23–24
Sikhs, 93
SL v Commission Scolaire des Chênes 2012 SCC 7, 79–80, **99**, 101
Steinbach Christian High School, 21, 39–40
Steinbach Regional Secondary School, 20, 43
Steinbach United Church, 44
stress, 3
substantive equality, **87**, 88
suicide and suicidal ideation, 42, 72–73
Sukkot, Jewish festival of, 28–29
Supreme Court of Canada: on Catholicism, 121–22; on *Charter* rights, 12–13, 25; on competing rights claims, 11; on freedom of religion, 16, 23, 30, 33, **99**, 117–18, **118**; on inclusion of 2SLGBTQ+ individuals, 98–99; on minority rights, 100; on parent decisions, 79, 112–13; on religion, 94–95; on schools, **81**, 82; on sexual orientation, 26–27, 89, 133; on Surrey School Board case, 66; *Syndicat Northcrest v Anselem*, 29; Trinity Western University and, 14, **24**, 28, 35–36
Surrey, British Columbia, 66
Surrey School Board, 66
surveillance cameras, 51, 52
Syndicat Northcrest v Anselem 2004 SCC47, 28–29, **29**, 30, 90–91, 94–95

teachers: conduct of, 117–19; disqualifying, 120–21; governing bodies of, 121; support from, 37, 55, 115, 131; training for, 56. *See also* administrators; principals
Teens Educating and Confronting Homophobia (T.E.A.C.H.), 124
Thunder Bay, Ontario, 45
Toews, Vic, 31
tolerance, **24,** 57, 101, 132
Tourloukis, Dr. Steve, 102–3, 112–13, 125
training, for teachers, 56
transgender identities and students, 3–5, 16–17, 38–39, 95, 96–97, 107–9
transitioning, 109
transphobia, 42, 53, 72, 128–29, 132
Trinity Western University (TWU), 14, **24,** 66
Trinity Western University v British Columbia College of Teachers 2001 SCC 31, **24**
true self, 4, 21–22
truth, **89,** 119

Uganda, 85
United Conservative Party (UCP), Alberta, 73, 74

Vancouver, British Columbia, 95, 109
Vancouver Catholic School Board, 109
Vancouver Rape Relief & Women's Shelter, 95
violence, physical, 52–53, 129, 131–32
voices of children and youth, 63–67, 97
Vriend v Alberta 1998 SCR 493, 89, 98–99

washrooms, 107–8, 109
Whatcott, Bill, 32–33, **33**
Wiebe, Scott, 21
Wiens, Evan, 20, 21–22, 31, 43, **43**
Wilson, Tracey, 38